Tales of the
Shopocracy

Tales of the Shopocracy

A portrait of my father and his world

John Barnie

Gomer

Acknowledgements

I would like to thank Ceri Wyn Jones at Gomer
for his sympathetic editing.
Chapter 24 first appeared in *The New Welsh Review*.

Published in 2009 by
Gomer Press, Llandysul, Ceredigion, SA44 4JL

ISBN 978 1 84851 068 5
A CIP record for this title is available from the British Library.

© Copyright text: John Barnie, 2009

John Barnie asserts his moral right under the
Copyright, Designs and Patents Act, 1988
to be identified as author of this work.

This book is published with the financial support of the
Welsh Books Council.

Printed and bound in Wales at
Gomer Press, Llandysul, Ceredigion

for Talfan

1

To his family and friends he was always Ted, but on his letterheaded invoice book he was E.C. Barnie, Wholesale and Retail Confectioner. He had opened the shop in the 1920s with £20 of capital borrowed from one of his brothers or sisters, all of whom were shopkeepers or had married shopkeepers – there was a stationer and newsagent's on the square in Monmouth, and a baker's; the village store and post office on the Mardy just outside Abergavenny; and the tobacconist and barber's run by his sister May and her husband Ernie Hodges, next door to the shop which my father rented from them until he retired in 1969.

The sweet shop was small. You entered through a narrow door into a space where six or seven customers formed a crowd. On the right were shelves that reached to the ceiling, lined with large glass sweet jars; on the left was the glass counter with displays of sweets and boxes of chocolates; more shelves stacked with screwtop bottles rose behind the narrow space where my father and mother stood day after day serving customers. There was an Avery scales on the counter for weighing out, and always a slab of toffee open in its white, waxy paper and a toffee hammer to break it up into brittle, shiny chunks. On hooks there were white paper bags of various sizes, including triangular ones that turned into cones when lemon sherbert was slipped rustling into them from the scoop. For years he bought his bags from Sergeants, the printers in Queen Street, whose big stone building with its glass roof and clattering machines timed the day for the town with hooters calling the printers to work, marking their lunch hour, and the end of the working day. Eventually, though, they became too expensive and my father turned to a firm in Bristol that was cheaper. In their small town way, he and my mother attributed Sergeants' decline (it took several decades) to that failure to hold their prices. 'You can't run a business like that.'

There was every kind of sweet in the shop: boiled sweets and lemon drops, striped brown-and-white and black-and-white humbugs, toffees and liquorice toffees wrapped in paper or squeaky cellophane, chocolate drops, hundreds-and-thousands, acid drops, sherbert, turkish delight, mintoes, glacier mints, liquorice allsorts. The shop was full of rainbow colours and there was a rich aroma compounded of all the sweets, especially when I went with my father on a Sunday and he unlocked the door onto its dimly lit interior and the rows on rows of faintly gleaming jars.

2

My father was born on 14th September 1902, the youngest of nine children, two of whom died in infancy. His father, John Henderson Barnie, was a Scot from a crofting family in Upper Lybster in Caithness. One of many children, he emigrated to the South Wales coalfield in the 1880s as an eighteen- or nineteen-year-old. He travelled with a crudely made iron-bound wooden trunk that contained all his belongings, lodging at first with a doctor in Brynmawr who was also a Caithness man. He got a job as a packman for a Brynmawr draper, tramping about with his wares in the coal-mining villages of the south-eastern valleys.

Before long, though, he joined the police force as a constable, serving in various rural areas in eastern Monmouthshire until he was promoted to sergeant, stationed at first in Abergavenny, then in Monmouth. I met an old man once in Abergavenny who said Sergeant Barnie always carried a swagger stick with which he'd been whacked more than once for misbehaving. At least in memory he didn't seem to mind.

It's hard to get a strong sense of my grandfather. In the few photographs of him he is always staring, unsmiling, straight into the camera, curly-haired as a young man, though in middle age the hair had receded above his serious eyes and thick, black moustache. There are a few stories my father remembered about him. How when stationed at Monmouth he always received a brace of pheasant at Christmas from the gamekeeper at the Rolls estate. (There is a photograph of him surrounded by a curious crowd, guarding one of Rolls's pioneer aeroplanes on Monmouth race course in 1912. He is an image of authority.) My father told, too, how in the early years of the First World War he and his older brother Bill were playing 'trenches' in the garden and Bill shot my father in the forehead with an air rifle. He could have killed him, and when my father stumbled into the house, his face covered in blood, John Henderson picked up a loaf my grandmother had been soaking to make bread-and-butter pudding and flung it at the ceiling.

He was strictly religious, a Congregationalist (his wife, who came from an English farming family, was Church of England), and a teetotaller who disapproved of gambling. All his sons became determined small-time gamblers on the horses and later football pools. Don, the eldest, had a hiding place behind a loose brick in the outside toilet where he kept his betting slips and winnings. Their father never found out, though they had to dodge him on Monmouth race course when he was there on duty during race meetings and they were there as well, placing bets. Sometime later, Don and Bill set out to make a living as professional gamblers, travelling from course to course. They gave up after their kitty was stolen in a public lavatory in London. Bill had taken off his coat with the money in it to have a wash and brush up, and a sneak thief rifled the pockets, so they said.

Even on a sergeant's wages, times were lean. Apart from the trunk, one of the few artefacts connected with John Henderson is a small black-covered book in which he kept a weekly account of income and expenditure. Several times he notes that he has had to borrow from May, my father's sister's, piggy bank. John Henderson kept chickens and a couple of pigs as an essential addition to the family income. One of my father's jobs as a child was to collect buckets of acorns in the woods in autumn for pig feed. He earned a penny a bucket. When the butcher came to slaughter a pig, my father had to kneel with a bucket to catch the blood from its slit throat, stirring the blood to stop it clotting while the pig squealed and struggled as it was held down on a table. Later the blood was made into black pudding.

John Henderson was not very good at killing. There is a story of how one day he went to butcher a hen for dinner. He placed its neck across a chopping block and cut the head off with one blow of a hatchet. The headless bird ran blundering down the garden till it dropped dead. He never slaughtered another hen himself. This and his exasperated reaction to Bill almost killing my father (after splattering the ceiling of the kitchen with sopping bread, John Henderson took the air rifles and smashed them against a tree) suggests a more sensitive man than you would guess from the stern image in the photographs. Perhaps there was a sensitivity there which his upbringing made it impossible to express, except in extreme situations when it came out as anger.

After many years, he managed to save enough money to make the long journey home to Caithness to see his parents. When he reached Edinburgh, however, a telegram overtook him, saying that Bill had run away to sea. He took the train back to South Wales and eventually tracked his son down in Bristol. What was said between them is not known; nor is it known why Bill ran away. John Henderson never returned to Scotland and never saw his parents again.

3

What my father was like as a child is hard to gauge, though from what I knew of him later, I suspect he would have been shy. Here too he can only be followed through a series of disconnected stories. One Christmas as a very small child he was given a Noah's Ark with pairs of wooden animals; but Noah himself was missing. When my father discovered this early on Christmas morning he was inconsolable and John Henderson had to go and wake the shopkeeper who lived above the shop in Monmouth to retrieve the Noah.

Another story tells how my father was run over as a five- or six-year-old by a horse and cart; not under the wheels presumably but tangled up in the horses' hooves. He wasn't hurt but he never forgot the experience. The story illustrates the speeded-up history of the twentieth century. My father was born into a world of horse transport where an automobile still had to have a man with a red flag walking before it; he remembered the Rolls' car being driven through Monmouth in this way. There was also the Rolls' experimental plane that he saw as a child in primary school rising a few feet off the ground on the race course, then sputtering down to an awkward landing; perhaps the same plane that his father guarded in the photograph. Yet by the end of his life the roads were choked with cars, aeroplanes flew at supersonic speeds across the Atlantic, and the Americans had landed on the Moon.

Another tale tells how my father, again aged five or six, was sitting on the rim of the water butt, swinging his legs. He lost his balance and tipped over backwards into the water. He would have drowned but for the quick action of a neighbour who found him and hauled him out and revived him. Telling the tale again, my father would laugh gently to himself as he warmed his hands at the kitchen fire.

In Monmouth the police sergeant lived in the Old Gaol and my father's bedroom had been the condemned cell with a small high window criss-crossed with iron bars as thick as an arm. He met an old man once who recalled seeing the last public hanging in the town when he was a boy.

No other tales have come down and in fact my father's childhood was short because in 1915 John Henderson died. My father remembers him retching up a bilious green liquid from his mouth. It must have been a frightening time and a worrying one for his mother, Martha. John Henderson was only in his fifties and might have been expected to live many more years. His death meant that life became very insecure. In 1915 the Great War was bogged down in Flanders, and Don, the eldest son, was with the Royal Welch Fusiliers fighting at Gallipoli. As the Old Gaol was a tied police house, the family had to move out and my father left school aged thirteen to make a living. I'm not sure what happened to his mother, but I suspect she went to stay with one of her daughters who would have been married by then.

Later, and certainly by the time of the Second World War, she moved to Abergavenny where she lived in two rooms above my father's shop. She died in 1947 when I was six. I remember visiting her with my mother, climbing the rickety wooden stairs at the back of the shop, through the 'kitchen' where she washed and cooked and where my father boiled up and emulsified his ice cream, into her cramped front sitting room. There was a room next door which was her bedroom. The sitting room had a raised platform under the window which gave onto the street. I could stand there and look down in secret on the foreshortened passers-by. My grandmother always seems to have been dressed in black, at least in memory, with small round glasses, plump and tiny and totally alien to a five- or six-year-old. She let me play with her sewing basket while she and my mother chatted; I liked the reels of brightly coloured cotton. I have no other memories of her and didn't attend her funeral. In fact I was never taken to any of the family funerals even as a teenager. That was the work of my mother, who didn't like funerals herself and even made excuses when her oldest friend, Grace Shackleton, died in the 1980s. It was as if we had to avert our faces from the sight of death.

My grandmother's bedroom became a storeroom after she died, its curtains permanently closed to keep out the sun. Here were box on box of sweets and chocolates stacked on shelves, piled on the floor, and the smell was even more overpowering and delicious than in the shop. I used to go there to breathe it in, just as I'd go into the garage at home which had originally been a stables and still had a manger for the horse, and breathe in the rich scent of petrol from the accumulated layers of oily dirt beneath the car.

My father's first job was as an assistant at Tutt's the grocers in Monmouth. Again there are stories. Of how each Monday, he and the other assistants had to weigh out tea, sugar, coffee, flour, currants etc. into pound and half-pound paper bags from the barrels, tubs and tins in which they were stored. There's a tale of how one day the assistants played a trick on an old orthodox Jew, placing his weekly order on top of a barrel of lard. When he came in, black-coated and hatted, with a long grey beard, and saw the lard, he ran out of the shop shouting 'Voi! Voi! Voi!' It is not recorded whether they got a row.

There seems to have been an atmosphere of fun at Tutt's as well as hard work. Every new apprentice would be sent to the ironmongers at some point to buy 'half a dozen sky hooks, please', and my father remembered standing in the cellar of the shop one day with another assistant looking up at a woman who stood on the grating above. This was in 1915 or 1916 when women still wore dresses down to their ankles. To the boys' surprise, she started peeing through the grating while she casually examined the contents of the window. Sometimes by being below you see things you would otherwise miss.

Hours would have been long and he would have worked every day except Sunday, with a half-day off on early closing day. At 1pm every shop in town would close, blinds pulled down over the windows if it was summer, the long winding main street utterly empty like a deserted set for a Western. It seemed as if everybody was asleep, which most of the shopkeepers probably were, before rousing themselves and going out reluctantly to mow the lawns. The purr and rattle of mechanical lawnmowers was the soporific background to an otherwise soundless afternoon even when I was a child, there being almost no traffic in the streets in the 1940s or early 1950s.

After he moved to Abergavenny, my father would cycle on early closing day the seventeen miles to Monmouth to see his mother and hand over part of his wages. Then he would cycle the seventeen miles back, ready for work next day.

4

When I was growing up almost all the families we knew ran shops. There were Shackletons the chemists who lived across from us on the Hereford Road, and, next door to them, Williamses the greengrocers – Mrs Williams and Mrs Shackleton were sisters with whose daughters I played as a four- or five-year-old. Two doors down lived the owner of a gents' outfitters with his wife and daughter. They were talked about in hushed tones, because he was an alcoholic. The shop had been founded by his father, but the son was busy wrecking it. There were reports that customers had found empty gin and vodka bottles among the racks of overcoats. My parents had a theory that it started during the Second World War when he had been an officer in the RAF. He had felt socially inferior in the officers' mess, the theory went, and this had caused him to drink in an effort to boost his self-confidence. I'm not aware that there was any evidence for this, but once formulated, it became the explanation for his small-town destructive fate, and no other possible cause was ever discussed.

It had the advantage of explaining his behaviour in terms the shopocracy could understand. As shopkeepers, my father and his siblings were upwardly mobile. It was a step up from having a father who was employed as a policeman to being your own man. A shop gave standing in the community, but it was an insecure standing. For the most part poorly educated (Mr Shackleton, a trained pharmacist, was an exception), they had started out with nothing, and had achieved their independence through years of dogged hard work. Someone like Mr L——, the men's clothier, disturbed them because here was one of their kind behaving recklessly, a shopkeeper who was out of control, who revealed through his behaviour his inner demons, something you should never do. So Mr L—— and his family were talked about, by the women over tea, by the men in the Conservative Club. 'It's poor Betty I feel sorry for.'

Because they came up from nothing (again Mr Shackleton was one of the few exceptions; he inherited the chemist's from his father), they craved respect and sought it in respectability. This meant voting Conservative, upholding religion, never getting into debt ('if you can't afford something, save up for it or go without'), never telling other people your business, providing your children with a better education than you had so they could 'get on'. They craved security. Those of my generation who were the first from the shopocracy to go to university were urged to get a 'secure' job, in teaching for example. My cousin John Hodges who taught French in a grammar school in Birmingham was held up as the model. He had 'got on'.

There was no real security in shopkeeping and there were many roads to ruin, as they knew from within the family. Don's store and post office on the Mardy never really thrived. He was, according to my parents, too soft, giving in to villagers' hard luck stories and letting them buy groceries on the slate. 'You can't run a shop like that.' When he was dying of cancer in the mid-1950s, the store can't have been bringing in much; it was sold at a knockdown price shortly before he died. Then on my mother's side there was Uncle Fred Wood whose bakery went more or less bankrupt. He sold out to his rivals, Alderton's, and all the time I knew him he worked for them as a roundsman, taking a van out six days a week into the country around the town. It was that kind of downward mobility they feared. Nobody ever said Uncle Fred was inferior, but he and his wife and daughter were poor, and that is what happened when you went over the edge or when softheartedness clouded your business sense. 'Neither a borrower nor a lender be' was their motto.

The shopkeepers were highly class conscious. They were, at

17

best, on the lower rungs of the bourgeoisie and they knew it. They were the backbone of the petite bourgeoisie, though they would never have used that term or known what it meant if they heard it. Above them, and treated with a kind of distant respect, was the professional class of doctors, solicitors, teachers, the town librarian. The shopkeepers never mixed socially in those circles, even in the Conservative Club (the Constitutional Club as it declared itself above the main entrance; the Con Club as members called it without irony) which my father belonged to. Members were drawn mostly from the shopocracy and from upwardly mobile elements among the town's working class, but there was a sprinkling of solicitors and other professionals among them who formed their own elite in the men-only bar and snooker room. You might exchange a bit of banter with them, but you never made up a foursome over the tables.

Above the professionals were the landed gentry and various prosperous middle class individuals who didn't fit into the professional niche but whose evident wealth, proclaimed in their grand houses on streets like Avenue Road, gave them a status of their own. Some of them were regular customers at my father's shop. I wouldn't say they were given special treatment, but they were treated with deference, especially by my mother. My father, I think, was more indifferent to them; it was my mother who brought them into conversation from a treasured hoard of anecdotes. There was Mrs So-and-So from Gilwern, a wealthy widow, who regularly bought a whole tin of toffees for her dogs, and Sir Harry Llewelyn's housekeeper who came in every week with an order. Once, my mother was invited by her to look over Sir Harry's mansion when he and the family were away. It was a talking point for years. There was no 'side' to such people. The shopocracy was constantly on the look-out for 'side' and reacted to it strongly. One country gent in the 1930s would park his car outside the shop and toot his horn, expecting my father to come out and serve him. He was told 'in no uncertain terms' that if he

18

wanted serving he had to come into the shop like everyone else. My mother always told this story, not my father, though sitting in front of the fire with his hands on his knees, he would chuckle and nod. It was one up for the shopocracy whose pride could only be challenged so far.

My father, who had been a member of the Conservative Club from its foundation in the 1920s, went there every evening, except Sunday, at 9 o'clock. He and my mother would get back from the shop at 6pm when we would have tea; usually a boiled egg and white bread and butter, or scrambled eggs or baked beans on toast. Dinner was at 1 o'clock when the shop would be closed for an hour, except on market days. After tea my father would settle down in the 'dining room', where we never dined, with the evening paper, *The South Wales Argus*, and we would listen to the radio. *Dick Barton, Special Agent* was my favourite at 6.45 every weekday evening; there was also the half-hour *Journey into Space* at 7.30 and *The Goon Show*. My parents would listen to *The Billy Cotton Band Show* and *Henry Hall's Guest Night*, variety shows that mixed big band dance music and (in the case of Billy Cotton) amiable comedy. Some years later, *Dick Barton* was replaced by *The Archers* and we listened to that. They also liked Saturday's *In Town Tonight* which began with the sound of traffic, engines revving and the tooting of horns, then the chimes of Big Ben summoning up far-away and unimaginable London. It was a proto chat show in which what we would now call celebrities appeared who were 'in town'. 'Town', I learned, was always London. My mother's friend Mrs Shackleton would sometimes go 'up to town' to see a 'show', meaning a musical, coming back the same day on the late train. This seemed amazingly glamorous and daring. It gave the Shackletons an edge among the shopocracy; they were our elite. It was no surprise when they became the first in our circle to go on a cruise and to own a ciné camera. I remember us all going over to the Shackletons to see the film of their Mediterranean cruise. Shaky hand-held panoramas of sea

19

and sky taken from the Rock of Gibraltar; Mrs Shackleton gazing at the view, trying to seem unaware of the camera, then turning, as if surprised, and giving a forced smile and a little wave of the hand.

Perhaps my father would doze a bit while the radio was on, then at nine he would stretch and say 'Well, I'm off to the Club' and go out into the hall for his mack and trilby. Later, when I was a student, I would go with him, down through Bailey Park if it was summer and the Park still open, or along the dimly lit, crooked lane by the side of the Park if it was winter, hemmed in by the green-painted railings on one side, and the high sandstone walls of the cattle market and the slaughter house with its smells of offal and dried blood on the other. Sometimes you would hear cows lowing or pigs squealing inside the gaunt, echoing building as they waited in their pens for slaughter the following day.

My father would open one of the big wooden doors of the Club and we would push through the inner glass-panelled swing doors to enter the warm fug of beer and cigarette smoke, the quiet hubbub of the voices of the town's small-time Conservatives. There was a lounge immediately to the left where Bill Shackleton always perched or stood at the bar with his friends, but we never went in there. Instead we turned into the second door which brought us round to the other side of the bar and the club's snooker room with its two green-baize tables glowing under canopied lights slung on chains from the ceiling. Brightly coloured snooker balls would be spread across the baize, or someone would be setting up, gathering the red balls into their wooden triangle and placing the apex expertly just behind the spot for the pink. If a table was free, I would be delegated to occupy it while my father made his way through the gaggle of men around the bar to get us a beer.

I was always slightly embarrassed going to the Club. I wasn't a member and my father had to sign me in as a guest (or he should have done; in practice he rarely bothered). I would never be a member either but since I was about eleven we had had a quarter-size snooker table in the large front room and I had learned to play. Sometime after I turned eighteen my father had the idea of taking me for a game at the Club, and this we did regularly whenever I was home from university. After the quarter-size table at home, the Club's tables seemed huge, an immense expanse of green for the balls to speed across, clicking into each other, thudding into the rubber-protected cushion of the sides, or disappearing soundlessly and satisfyingly into one of the pockets.

Neither my father nor I was very good but we were competent enough in his circle of players where we would often make up a foursome if the tables were busy. As he got older, my father's game got worse. 'That's a bad 'un,' he would say, his lower lip protruding in a pout, almost before he had hit the cue ball. 'I'm giving this game up.' But when I made a break he would say proudly 'You could be good if you only practised.' Once or twice he urged me to join the Conservative Club in Birmingham where I was at university to get access to their tables, but he must have known that I wouldn't.

The Con Club was a world of male camaraderie. When women, or 'ladies', were allowed in, it was strictly upstairs. They were never to enter the bar or snooker room. I don't think my mother ever went through the Club's doors, though Mrs Shackleton did, for whatever 'do' it was that wives persuaded their husbands to escort them to.

Eleven o'clock was closing time, and my father would be back in the house by 11.20 with the stale smell of beer on his breath, though he was never a big drinker. When, later on, I went with him, he would have two half pints at most. He told the story of the only time in his life that he had got drunk. It was on Armistice Day, 1918, when he was sixteen and had been out celebrating the end of the War with the rest of the town. My father had lodgings in Ross Road then, and when he went out of the front door the following day to go to work, he felt so dizzy and ill that he had to clutch the iron railings in front of the house and stumble back in. It 'taught him a lesson' and he never got drunk again. My mother too hardly drank; a glass of sweet sherry, or a Babycham – the shopocracy's champagne, with a glacé cherry spiked on a cocktail stick – was her limit. We only ever had alcohol in the house at Christmas when there would be brown flagons of beer for the men, a bottle each of Gordon's gin, Captain Morgan rum and Bell's or Teacher's whisky, and a refillable soda syphon for the whisky drinkers. While the rum lasted, my father liked an occasional rum toddy before going to bed – a measure of rum in a glass with a teaspoon of sugar and hot water. It smelled delicious to me as a child. A rum toddy was what the adults drank at midnight on New Year's Eve, my father coming in just in time from the kitchen with a tray of steaming glass tumblers.

5

Christmas was one of the busiest times in the shop. My father ran
a Christmas Club into which customers paid a small amount each
week. As Christmas neared, they would place orders for sweets,
boxes of chocolates and Christmas crackers, and these would be
wrapped and piled up in the ice-cream parlour ready for
collection. My father also delivered and on several evenings in the
week before Christmas I would go with him in the car, usually up
to the housing estate below the Deri, knocking on doors and
delivering parcels to open arms, children watching in the lighted
hall. At least until the end of the 1950s he also supplied a number
of corner shops up in the Valleys. I went with him once, the old
Standard 13 climbing laboriously through Clydach Gorge and
Black Rock, then down into the mining villages. I had never been
to the Valleys before, and it was a shock. Every village seemed
composed of long rows of drab houses strung across the valley's
sides above the winding gear of the mines and huge slag heaps like
dismal pyramids. On the valley floor a railway line snaked with
coal wagons. Smoke and steam drifted aimlessly. In the early
1950s there were very few cars in Abergavenny; none of the
teachers at the Grammar School had one; but in these mining
villages there were no cars at all, and there was nothing except
gaunt, empty streets which the Standard 13 nosed along, coming
to a halt outside a tiny shop. I was painfully aware of our special
status in owning a car, and when I sometimes got a lift back to
school after dinner, I would make sure that my father dropped me
some way from the gates. Here, it might have been Nant-y-glo,
the car and what it stood for was even more obvious, and I saw it
reflected in the hostile stare of the few lean men who hung about

on street corners. I felt acutely uncomfortable, and only relaxed when we began the descent of Black Rock into the Usk valley. The rampart of the Blorenge and Llangattock Mountain became a symbolic barrier between me and the industrial south. My world was the green world of the Usk and the Black Mountains, a world despised as soft in the Valleys, and it was many years before I went there again.

For a shopkeeper, estimating how much stock to buy is a constant problem. My father, who was a worrier, was always cautious, but my mother through constant nagging persuaded him to overstock (as he saw it), especially at Christmas. So on cold November nights my father would lie awake in bed thinking about boxes of unsold and unsellable Christmas crackers and financial ruin. This might seem strange in a lifelong, small-time gambler, but it might be explained by the fact that when he bet on the horses or did the pools, he almost always lost. In this sense my mother was the real gambler, and a successful one, because every Christmas they sold out and could have sold more. This made my mother more reckless the following year when she would persuade my father to put in an even bigger order and he would lie awake in bed worrying again.

6

During the football season, Littlewood's pool forms would be filled out each week, my father setting his crosses and noughts down with a blue biro, his tongue extended between his lips in concentration. The form, and the cost of his bet in coins, were then sealed in a Littlewood's envelope to be collected by the agent who every Tuesday evening went from door to door. On Saturday we would listen to the 6 o'clock news on the radio and my brother and I would have to sit in silence while the announcer gave out the scores. My father sat, tongue out again, checking his coupon. I don't remember him having enough draws to win anything, though I suppose he must have now and then. If we went up to the Mardy on Sunday, my father and his brother Don would always compare notes. 'Aye, Leeds let me down. I was sure they were going to draw.'

It was the same with the horses, though there he did have more luck, getting a double or treble up which brought in a few pounds. In their younger days before the Second World War, he and Don sometimes went to the races in Hereford or Chepstow. After their marriage, my mother would go with them now and then. Again there are tales. How Don and my father studied form and how my mother, who knew nothing about horses, bet on a name she found attractive or on a horse that looked 'nice' in the paddock. At one meeting she bet on Shinley Goldenheart in the first race, to the scorn of Don and Ted. It was a rank outsider. But the favourites fell and Shinley Goldenheart came trundling home to win. She won the following two races as well, and my father and Uncle Don ended up looking over her shoulder to see what she was going to do next.

Then there is the tale of the time Don and my father won big-time for them – two or three hundred pounds; and how they stopped the car on the way back from the course and bought bottles of champagne. The time too when they encountered a fog so thick that they couldn't see the side of the road and ended up in a farmyard. These were the high times of the shopocracy when they were still young; before the children came, in my parents' case; before the War which changed everything.

The routine of my father's gambling had a strange effect on me which I can't explain. Sitting on the floor in the dining room on Saturdays as the winter sky darkened outside, listening to the litany of team names and scores, or the results at the race meetings, I came to detest the world of sport. Sometimes my father would listen to a radio broadcast of a football match or race meeting on the radio, and I would be playing beneath the macho roar of the crowd, the intense excitability of the commentator – 'And he's *scored*! *What* a goal!' – and I hated it, for its drab, irreducible masculinity. For the dull predictability of it all, because the small-time gambler's world re-enacts the myth of Sysiphus again and again and again. Hated it because it was what defined masculinity in this world and it left me cold. For the same reason I dreaded Wednesday afternoons in winter which was sports afternoon at the Grammar School. Then we would have to change into our rugby kit – all blue for the Rusticans, the boys from the country; blue shorts with a red shirt for the Oppidans, town boys like me. Off we went through the back gate of the school and round past the Fair Field to Bailey Park, where we played on the muddy, boot-studded pitch, me trying to position myself where the ball wasn't likely to land, but forced into the scrums where I was a prop forward, the position given to anyone who showed no aptitude for the game. In Sixth Form, I was allowed to switch to cross-country running along the lower slopes of the Deri, and in summer I substitued tennis for cricket. Tennis in the 1950s was suspect. It was played by the town's middle class at the

Pen-y-pound Tennis Club, and walking past in the evening you could hear their plummy calls, 'Oh well played, Tommy!' Tennis was sissy and for girls, and if caught walking with a tennis racket, you might get jeered at. So I always felt self-conscious about it. Once on the public courts at Bailey Park, though, I was free.

My father never played any sport in his life, except snooker and darts, which weren't really considered sports then. But every Saturday evening in winter, 'Quiet now, it's the results', and the dull BBC voice would announce 'Liverpool – 0, Wolverhampton Wanderers – 1; Leeds United – 2, Sheffield Wednesday – 2' and to make what seemed an interminable time pass, I tried to guess from the inflexion of the voice whether the second team had won, drawn or lost, while my father leaning forward, biro in hand, read defeat in the blue grid of the coupon.

7

The other busy time in the shop was summer. From the beginning of June to the end of August, my father made and sold his own ice cream. You could buy a wafer or a cone to take out, or you could have a more elaborate ice cream and eat it in the parlour, the room behind the shop which was laid out with cheap wooden tables, chairs and stools, with a gangway through the middle for staff. Behind the parlour was a rather shabby area with a high lean-to roof that sloped away from the main building. There was a washstand on the left and at the far end a toilet. My father had killed a rat there once when the sewers had backed up during a flood. To the right was the wooden stairs leading to the upper storerooms and my grandmother's room. Just by the stairs was a space where cardboard boxes and other packing material was piled higgledy-piggledy, to be put out for the bin men each week. At the top of the stairs there was a small landing and a window on the left which gave onto a secret Abergavenny, a world of ancient, patched-up roofs and guttering and tottery-looking chimneys. I liked to look out on this scene of slow, collapsing decay which the serene shop fronts concealed.

My father had made ice cream from the beginning, at first on a small scale with a machine that was something like a butter churn; the ice-cream mixture was poured into the churn which was sealed and then hand-churned until the mixture eventually thickened and crystallised. The churn itself was packed in a cannister of chemicals which induced the mix to freeze. It was a long and laborious process. By the time I knew him, the shop had industrial-scale stainless steel fridges in the third upstairs room, and vats and an emulsifier in the 'kitchen'. The ice-cream making facilities were inspected regularly by the food inspectors looking for salmonella, but my father always passed their tests. I doubt he would today, supposing anyone was foolish enough to make his own ice cream commercially. Even with the modern equipment he had acquired by the late 1940s, it was hard work. Six days a week, he would be down at the shop by 6.30 in the morning to prepare the mix, boiling it and emulsifying it, then pouring it into stainless steel cannisters eighteen inches in diameter and about three feet in depth. These were heavy in themselves and very heavy when filled with liquid ice cream that had to be humped to the fridges in the other room. There is a story, told by my mother, that once he slipped and poured a whole cannister over himself and the floor. His glasses were smeared with the mixture and the floor was so slippery that every time he tried to get up he slipped and fell down again. Listening to this by the fireside, my father would chuckle. It must have been a depressing day at the time, though – all that work gone to waste, the linoleum floor to clean up, and the process to be started over again. Once the ice-cream mix was safely in the fridges, my father came home for a quick breakfast, then back to the shop to open up at 8.30 to catch the town's boys and girls on their way to school.

The ice cream had to be kept at just the right temperature. Too high, and it would become runny. Too low, and it would set in an icy mass that you couldn't dip a scoop in. Once it was set, the big cannisters had to be manhandled through the kitchen, down the stairs, through the parlour and into the shop. There, at right angles to the counter, was another long fridge with three circular spaces for the cannisters which were lowered in carefully and covered with stainless steel lids. At the side was a scoop ready to be dipped for a hemisphere of the thick, creamy ice cream. The scoop was inverted over a cone; then you pressed a lever which passed a band of steel around the inside of the scoop and the ice cream slipped easily into the mouth of the cone. There was another, rectangular device for making wafers. You loaded it with a couple of scoops and flattened them out with a knife until the space was filled, then you inverted it over a wafer and pressed a plunger in the handle which squeezed the ice cream out in a perfect rectangle.

Just before the ice-cream season, my father would buy several large sheets of stiff white card, get the stencil set from under the stairs, and stencil in bright colours the adverts for this year's ice cream which would hang outside the shop. 'Barnie's Home-made Ice Cream', they would declare. Apart from cones and wafers to take out, you could also 'Try Our Ice Cream Parlour' where customers could sit down to a Polar Ice – two wafers stacked on top of each other, then coated with cream, and criss-crossed with a lattice of molten chocolate. Home-made raspberry sauce was spooned around the base. (A variation on the cone was the Choc Ice with dark molten chocolate that froze into a gleaming cap, crackling in the mouth as you ate it.)

In the parlour, you could also have the more expensive Knickerbocker Glory. A scoop of ice cream was dropped into the well of a tall, slim glass with a fluted lip. Slivers of peach, home-canned, were added, together with some of the sweet, viscous juice from the can; then another scoop of ice cream, then more peaches and so on to the top which was finished off with spoonfuls of cream and a pair of wafers gently pressed into the last scoop of ice cream. This was served in the parlour on a plate, with a long spoon so you could reach the bottom of the glass.

My father's ice cream was very popular. It was rich and creamy and unlike any other ice cream I have tasted. Years after my parents had retired and my father was dead, people would come up to my mother in the street and say 'Oh Mrs Barnie, we do miss your ice cream'. One customer asked if she could have, and was given, the recipe for the raspberry syrup. My father was proud of his ice cream and its reputation, but making it and serving it was hard work.

In the 1950s fruit was still seasonal, and in September, when peaches were in season, my father would order thirty or more crates from Ruther's, the greengrocer and fishmonger in Frogmore Street. These would be delivered by Ruther's van to the back door of our house and stored in the lean-to conservatory (though we called it a greenhouse) at the side. The following Sunday, my parents' one free day in the week, the kitchen was turned over to the production of canned peaches. My mother would boil up large quantities of 'syrup' – sugar dissolved in water. In a separate saucepan, water was kept simmering and the peaches would be dropped into it one by one to blanch. After a few seconds in the pot they were taken on trays to the kitchen table where the loosened skins were prized off to reveal the gleaming, yellow fruit, oozing with juice. This was then circled with a knife and cut in half, and the crinkly stone carefully removed with a grapefruit knife. The halves were passed on to my mother or father who cut them into slices and packed them in canning tins. Once packed, the slices were covered to the lip of the tin with syrup and the can was placed in the canning machine which resembled a tin opener in reverse. A lid was placed over the can and, at the turn of a handle, the machine welded the two together in an air-tight seal. As the day wore on, the pile of sealed cans grew until they were taken to the wash house, an outhouse behind the scullery, where my father had lit the gas under my mother's big galvanised-iron washing tub. The cans were plunged into the boiling water and left to gurgle and rattle among themselves. When they were taken out, the lids were inspected. If they remained slightly depressed, the cans were good. If they had domed ever so slightly, there was air in them and they had to be abandoned. Most of the cans were good.

I enjoyed canning days. There was a lot of bustle and a holiday atmosphere. The kitchen and scullery were steeped in the aroma of peaches; piles of shed skins and stones gleamed golden yellow, the stones threaded with cotton-like strands of red. Box after box was brought in from the greenhouse with addresses in Spain stencilled on their sides. We had an espaliered peach tree on the south-facing wall of the house which my father had planted. It grew to about twenty feet and produced small fruit each year, which we ate, though they were not good enough for canning. The big juicy peaches of Spain were three times the size.

The cans were stored in a cupboard in the kitchen in silver rows where they stayed through the winter and spring until June came round and it was ice-cream season again.

Donald Barnie, Wick, c. 1882.

JOHNSTON, WICK.

John Henderson Barnie, Wick, c. 1882.

John Henderson Barnie, Swansea, c. 1883-4.

Martha Barnie (née Hale), Swansea, c. 1883-4.

John Henderson Barnie, c. 1895.

Marriage of Jessie Barnie with Charles Howes, c. 1905, outside the Old Gaol, Monmouth. Far right, seated, Martha and John Henderson Barnie. Far left, seated on the ground, Ted Barnie.

Ted Barnie as a 14-year-old in 1916.

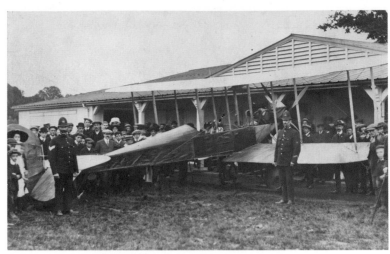

John Henderson Barnie (the police sergeant on the left) guarding the Rolls's biplane at Monmouth race course, 1912.

Larking about on the Maddocks's farm. Melva Barnie in the middle, c. 1925.

8

Because of the ice cream, we could never take a family holiday that coincided with the school holidays. We always went in the first two weeks of September instead, and every year my mother would write to the Headmaster asking if my brother and I could be excused from the first week of the autumn term. During the War and for several years afterwards, there were no holidays, but in the late 1940s we started going to Blackpool every year, staying at Mrs Tetley's boarding house a few streets from the sea front. She had strict rules: after breakfast, guests had to vacate the house and not return until 'high tea'. I remember Blackpool as windy and cold and the long sandy beach bleak and unwelcoming. But we stuck it out for several years into the early 1950s. I don't know what my parents did in the evenings after my brother and I had gone to bed, though once we all went to a theatre to a 'variety show'. The star was Jimmy Jewel who did a stand-up comedy act. We used to listen to his radio programme with Ben Warris and this is what must have led my parents to the unprecedented step of going to a theatre. There was also the ageing Irish tenor Josef Locke. He came on dressed a bit like a Mexican with a shiny cummerbund, throwing his arms out in large gestures to the audience as his voice throbbed with emotion, finishing with the song that had made him famous – 'Hear my song Vio-le-hett-aaah' – to prolonged applause. The backdrop showed a Mediterranean scene (or a Mexican one) with blue sea, white villas and a donkey, while the stage was bathed in a golden light that made everything that happened on it hyper-real and exciting. It is not known what my parents thought of it. They probably enjoyed it, or at least my mother did. My father never went to the theatre again though, as far as I know.

In this, the males of the shopocracy tended to be more conservative than the women. It was Mrs Shackleton who went up to town to see a show with her sister Vera Williams or my (much-older-than-me) cousin, Dorothy Gwenlan. Mr Shackleton, to my knowledge, stayed at home. Elite of the shopocracy as they were, though, Mr and Mrs Shackleton both took part in the Abergavenny Amateur Operatic Society's annual production at the Town Hall Theatre. This was always an operetta or a musical. My mother would go to see them, but never my father. I was persuaded to tag along once to *The Desert Song*. It was strange seeing people I knew step out of themselves, dressed as passionate sheiks and yearning maidens who launched into song at the slightest excuse. The more extrovert members of the shopocracy were the backbone of the Society, appropriating the leading roles.

This is as close as most of the shopkeepers got to 'culture', which would always have had a capital C in their minds, on the rare occasions when they thought about it. The more conservative among them might also have muttered something about putting on airs – most of the shopocracy were too entrenched in their role in small-town life ever to go outside of themselves in this way. To put on grease paint, wear funny clothes and, even worse, sing, was to invite ridicule which most of the shopocracy avoided at all cost. In this sense, the Shackletons were plucky and exuberant. The rest of us watched them cautiously from a distance, like the goings-on of people who had crossed a line which, if persisted in, would make them not one of us any more. After the two evenings' performances, though, Mr Shackleton would be back on his bar stool at the Con Club and Mrs Shackleton would be round for a coffee evening with my mother as if nothing had happened, though no doubt the women talked over the performance, as opposed to the men, most of whom hadn't seen it.

I don't know if my mother would have liked to have joined in. She was much more outgoing than my father, but there was never any talk of it that I can remember. Perhaps she didn't feel she had any talent for acting, though she had a voice and had taught herself to play the piano. Sometimes she would go into the front room where we had quite a good upright piano, and play and sing for half an hour, vamping out music hall and popular songs from the First World War and the 1920s, the time of her childhood and youth. Later, when as a teenager I began to learn blues piano, I ridiculed her sentimental performances and she stopped playing. It was part of a fumbling rebellion on my part against the town's petite bourgeoisie; against music as a class weapon.

From the age of twelve, I had been forced to go to piano lessons with Mr Wilcox, a bachelor who lived at the top of Hereford Road and made a living teaching piano to children like me in his front room. Once a week I would walk up the road to his house with my music case, take out the sheet music, and play whatever trial piece he had set for practice. This was my mother's idea, I think, not my father's, who didn't care about music one way or the other. But learning to play the piano was considered a social skill among the petite bourgeoisie and so I was put through my paces. I had to practise for fifteen minutes or so every evening after I had done my homework, my mother often sitting at my side on the piano stool, correcting me as I peered at the hideous squiggles, my fingers reaching out like dried sticks for the keys. It was worst in summer when the bay window of the front room would be open, and I could hear the shouts and screams of other children playing in the warm evening light.

I was a poor pupil, one of hundreds who must have ground down Mr Wilcox's love of music over the years, if he had any left by the time I met him. Eventually I was allowed to stop, forgot how to read basic notation and avoided the piano, until a few years later when I discovered the blues. Then, like my mother who couldn't read music either, I started to improvise by trial and error, one result of this being that my best key is 'B7'.

Later I regretted my hand in destroying my mother's delight in singing and playing – 'If you were the only/ girl in the world/ and

I was the only/ b-o-o-oy . . .', her left hand vamping on the bass, her right picking out the tune – and tried to persuade her to take it up again. But she never did.

By the mid-1950s, with rationing over, things were getting easier for the shopkeepers, and my parents abandoned Blackpool in favour of Bournemouth. There we stayed, not in a boarding house, but the Merville Hotel, a short distance from the promenade. This must have been a considerable expense for them. Built in the 1920s, it was painted a white that was blinding in the sunshine and could have been designed as a set for ITV's *Poirot*. Inside were thick pile carpets, a dining room reached through glass-panelled doors where guests were assigned tables for the duration of their stay. Waiters and waitresses wore black uniforms, the waitresses with little white aprons and lace caps. The Head Waiter (he was capitalised in our minds) stood austerely with his back to a sideboard on which was a wooden box marked 'Tronc'. He wore full evening dress and seemed to do nothing except touch a waiter on the sleeve now and then, pointing to a table that needed attention. At one end there was a dais for the band that played every Saturday evening, and a circular dance area set off from the herring-bone parquet floor.

The food must have been a basic variation on meat-and-two-veg (otherwise my father wouldn't have gone there), but there were exotica such as brown Windsor soup. 'Tip your plate away from you,' my mother would say. 'Why?' 'Because that's how it's done.' Afternoon tea was served in a basement where there was also a table-tennis table. The ball echoed harshly off the concrete walls which annoyed some of the guests, so there was a rule: no table tennis while tea was on.

Behind Reception, the saloon bar with its single full-size snooker table lay dim and empty during the day but was lit with subdued lighting in the evening. We boys weren't allowed in, but my parents went there after we had gone to bed. It was a mysterious place with the click-click-click of snooker or billiard

36

balls, murmured conversation, a barman glimpsed polishing a glass, with rows of coloured bottles repeated in the shining mirror behind him.

The bedrooms were large with high ceilings and you could order morning tea to be brought to your room. My brother and I had one room, my parents another next door; at eight o'clock a polite tap on the door brought in a uniformed maid with a tray, and teapot, cups, milk and sugar. She set this down on the bedside table with a 'Good morning' and went to draw the curtains.

This was all very strange, a world you weren't sure of, and it must have seemed so to my parents as well. It was a world where my mother tended to put on 'Abergavenny posh' in which a vase became a vawse; not to be one up on the staff but because she was uncertain of her own position. My father reacted by being shy, being less himself than usual. After a couple of holidays there, though, he began to relax and, deciding either that the early morning tea wasn't up to scratch or that it was too expensive (it could have been either), he brought along the primus stove we used on Sunday outings. Placing this inside a Huntley & Palmer's biscuit tin in the wardrobe, he brewed up with the battered picnic kettle, getting back in bed while it boiled. Other guests probably awoke to the piercing screech of the kettle's detachable whistle if he didn't get to it in time. My mother and we boys were embarrassed by this, but at least it was a proper cup of tea (he said). Before we went down to breakfast, windows had to be opened to get rid of the primus fumes and the tea-making paraphernalia secreted at the bottom of the wardrobe.

To us boys, Bournemouth was far better than Blackpool. The sun always seemed to shine for a start, and the sea was warm. In the morning we might stroll around the shops, my brother and I tugging in the direction of a brilliant toyshop that stocked lead soldiers, hand-painted cowboys and Indians on horseback, and yachts, their decks gleaming with varnish, with snow-white sails that could be raised or lowered on strings and a boom that swung out 90 degrees to catch the slightest ripple of breeze. My brother and I bought one each with our holiday money, and after the shops we either went to the beach or the ornamental gardens where there was a lake and an artificial stream where we could sail the yachts back and forth.

I doubt my father enjoyed these holidays very much. While we boys were straining to get to the toy shop, and my mother dawdled in front of dress-shop windows, my father walked on, trouser legs flapping, trilby cocked at the required angle, looking round occasionally to see if we were keeping up. One year, when I was deep into aircraft spotting, he was persuaded to take me to the nearby Farnborough Air Show. 'Oh you'll enjoy it Ted when you get there,' my mother had probably said. Packed in a crowd of several thousand spectators, I was in my element as each of the V-bombers – the Victor, the Valiant, and the delta-winged Vulcan – blasted their way a few hundred feet over our heads. A Canberra bomber was next, then the latest Hawker Hunter doing aerobatics, the last mark of the Meteor, shortly to be phased out of service, a helicopter backing and bowing over our upturned faces. I forgot about my father who hated crowds and noise and must have been in an agony of boredom and frustration. Eventually he unfolded a camping stool and sat down demonstrably and smoked. He must have seemed an odd air enthusiast to those around him. But these were planes I'd only seen in photos in *Flight International* which I bought at Smith's and nothing could spoil the excitement as the tannoy announced metallically '*And now the Mark II de Havilland Vampire soon to be brought into ser . . .*', the voice drowned out in crashing waves of the fighter's engine as it passed low overhead with thousands of people, except my father, craning up to look.

When we went on holiday, the shop was left in the hands of Nancy Legge, who had been an assistant for many years and remained so until my father retired. She came to his funeral when he died in 1981. This had always worked well, but after a few years my father decided that there was still too much trade in

September for Nancy to handle so that he, reluctantly, would have to forego the annual fortnight in Bournemouth. He drove us down, stayed for the day, then drove back to Abergavenny, picking us up a fortnight later. I'm sure that in those two weeks he enjoyed himself, napping in the evening, then going to the Club for a pint and a few games of snooker, gardening on Thursday afternoons and Sundays. He wasn't much of a cook, but that would have been a small price to pay.

The last family holiday was in 1957 when I was about to enter Sixth Form. I'm not sure why they ended then. Perhaps my mother had had enough of holidaying alone with us boys; it's hard to know what she did in the evenings at the Merville Hotel. Perhaps it was because I was beginning to drift out of boyhood and into other realms. At the end of the summer term, the English master at the Grammar School had given the two or three of us who were planning to study English in Sixth Form a small dark-blue hardback, *Three Augustan Poets*, a selection from Gray, Collins and Cowper, which was one of the set texts. It was a rite of passage, and although I understood almost nothing of the florid rhetoric of the poetry, I knew it was a turning point. Instead of sailing a toy yacht that year, I went on my own to hunt out a book shop, and there I bought T.S. Eliot's *Selected Poems* and *The Cocktail Party* in gloss-laminated Faber paperbacks. I didn't understand them either, but carried them around as if I could absorb their meaning through the skin.

For a while, though, we did continue Sunday outings, as we had done since I was a small child. Every Sunday in summer, my parents would discuss the weather and if it seemed promising would decide on where to go. Barry Island, as the nearest resort, was a favourite, more rarely Porthcawl. Later for some reason my parents extended the range, going as far as Ogmore and Southerndown. At Barry Island we would find a parking place in the big concrete garage-shelters where bus on bus brought trippers down from the Valleys. Early in the morning, my father had made piles of sandwiches with wafer-thin bread which only he could cut and butter (so my mother said). It was his one culinary skill, and encouraged by my mother, for whom it was one task less, he was rather proud of it. These were packed in greaseproof paper in a wicker basket that also contained cups and saucers, tea, sugar, a teapot and kettle, and milk in a small bottle corked with paper. The primus stove came in its Huntley & Palmer's biscuit tin. In the big Austin which we had by the mid 1950s we could also squeeze two deckchairs in the boot for my parents.

Despite working hard all week, my father enjoyed these outings more, I think, than the fortnightly holiday when he was taken out of his routine into enforced and unfamiliar idleness. At Barry Island, the deckchairs were lugged down the concrete steps past the cafeteria onto the beach where they were set up on as large a space as could be found on the crowded shore. While my brother and I changed and ran squealing into the sea, my parents would sit back smoking until my father tilted his trilby over his eyes and fell asleep. When we came back, all wet and sandy, he would trudge up to the car, boil the kettle on the primus in its tin, and return with the basket of food and a big brown pot of tea. Plates, cups and saucers would be pulled out and handed round, and we would sit and eat egg sandwiches, or salmon and cucumber, or ham and mustard. Then we boys would be off to build sandcastles near the tideline or to dunk in the waves again while my parents smoked and dozed surrounded by hundreds and hundreds of other groups like a noisy colony of terns.

Occasionally my mother would take off her shoes and come down and paddle in the wavelets, but I only remember my father doing this once or twice. I think my mother learned to swim when she was young, though paddling was her limit when I knew her. I doubt, though, whether my father had ever been more than up to his ankles in water outside his weekly bath.

My father had a strict dress code wherever he was and whatever he was doing. Always a suit, usually grey, with a sleeveless pullover if it was winter. Always braces, never a belt, and black shoes. In winter, long-johns, which in fact he only discarded in high summer, tucked into knee-length woollen socks. Always a thick vest, summer or winter. Outdoors, a trilby, again usually grey with a black hatband, cocked at a rakish angle. In the shop, he substituted the white knee-length confectioner's coat for the suit jacket which was hung on a hook upstairs in the 'kitchen'. Even when gardening, he wore a suit, an old one which my mother would have told him he couldn't possibly wear in public any more, so it became his gardening suit, with shoes and a trilby to match. Until well into the 1960s he wore shirts with detachable collars that had to be attached with a stud, back and front. The collars were starched and ironed by my mother so that they formed a very stiff, faintly gleaming curl. He would have gone on wearing them until he died, but the times were against him. In about 1964 he went to his gents' outfitters to get some replacement shirts. These always had a faint vertical stripe in pale brown or blue or green, and only three buttons from the neck down so that they had to be pulled over the head to get them on. 'Bloody hell, Ted, you're not still wearing those!' was the tailor's comment. After rummaging about, a pair or so were found, but they were the last. No one was making them any more, and he converted reluctantly to shirts with collars attached. There was always a tie, though, even on the beach in the heat of July and August. That was how the small-town shopkeepers of his generation dressed; it was unalterable and decades of fashion passed them by. In the Con Club everyone wore suits, though jackets might be taken off for a game of snooker. You could tell the solicitors by the gleam of satin or silk on the backs of their waistcoats as they stretched across the baize. Perhaps Mr Shackleton wore waistcoats, but it wasn't common among the shopkeepers.

The one exception to his dress code in all the years I knew him was the time he and my mother visited me shortly after I had gone to work in Denmark. It was a blistering Scandinavian August and it defeated my father. He abandoned his jacket and tie and even his vest and at my mother's insistence I took him into Copenhagen to buy a belt – 'You can't possibly go out looking like that with braces, Ted.' 'Why not?' Later that day we went to the beach at Hornbæk where, walking through the dunes, my father in shirtsleeves but with a trilby, we passed a young woman who was sunbathing topless. 'Now I've seen everything,' he whispered in my ear. And for a small-town shopkeeper, he probably had.

We didn't always go to the sea. Sometimes we drove to the Elan Valley and parked in a lay-by above the Claerwen dam. If for some reason my parents only wanted an afternoon trip we would drive up Fiddler's Elbow to picnic on the side of the Blorenge. Playing in the bracken and heather there, my brother and I found old unexploded mortar shells from the time it had been a firing range during the War. In August we would go to what was known as the Whinberry Hill, really the eastern slope of the Deri below the Sugar Loaf, where the whinberries were best. My parents took strawberry punnets or metal measuring jugs and soon were hidden in the deep bracken of the slope. There would be the pock-pock of whinberries until the bottom of the jug or punnet was covered, and then silence except for the occasional rustle of bracken as a picker moved on, or the insistent call of a stonechat. My brother and I would pick for a while and then go off to play Cowboys and Indians. Later in the week there would be whinberry tart for pudding with scoops of my father's ice cream. Wherever we were, at some point the primus stove in its biscuit tin would be brought out and the shrill whistle of the kettle would bring us boys careering down the slope.

Apart from picking whinberries, my parents' routine in the hills was the same as on the beach. Park, get out the deckchairs, sit back and smoke. What they came for was 'the view'. 'You can't beat Wales for scenery,' my mother would say. 'Why go anywhere else,' my father would add, thinking probably of the annual trek to Bournemouth. If it was windy or chilly my father would sit in the driver's seat of the car, looking down the Elan Valley, or across from the Blorenge to the misty blue-green of the Sugar Loaf and the Black Mountains. But that didn't last long, and cigarette between his fingers, he would take out the Sunday paper, turn to the page he wanted and fold it in half to read.

9

It's tempting to say that my parents weren't great readers. The only books in our house that were regularly consulted were a *Ready Reckoner* and a series of *Racing Almanacs* in their well-worn orange covers, and which were kept under the stairs. My mother had gone to the Abergavenny High School for Girls and had stayed till she was fifteen. She didn't read books but had come away from the High School with a residual reverence for literature. Once, when visiting relatives in Malvern as a little girl, she had passed George Bernard Shaw striding out over the hills and he had patted her on the head. I don't know how she knew it was him, but she was sure of it and often told the tale. It was a token of her bona fides; she may not have read books but she knew the worth of literature. She had kept some of her text books – an Everyman selection of essays down the centuries, a school edition of *A Midsummer-Night's Dream* which she had neatly signed 'Melva Fletcher III Remove' on the inside of the front cover. The book was published in 1923, her last year in school. She gave them to me when I was about to study English in Sixth Form; I hadn't known they existed. Apart from these there were only the books that I brought into the house – hardback Billy Bunters, Just Williams, The Famous Five, and later Bulldog Drummond, and anything I could find by John Masters and John Buchan. There was also a King James Authorised Version of the Bible which everyone was given a copy of on entering the Grammar School, and a leather-bound *Book of Common Prayer* which my aunt May Wood gave me when I was confirmed. These were kept in a drawer, a glove drawer I suppose, in the big wooden coat-and-hat stand in the hall, and were rarely taken out.

Apart from the *Racing Almanacs*, which were books you looked into for a horse's form, I don't think my father ever read a book after leaving school at thirteen, and what he might have read there is unknown and seemed to have left no impression on him. In this he was typical of the shopkeepers, none of whom had books in the house that I can remember. Later, in Sixth Form, when the English master, Wyn Binding, invited those of us studying English to his house in Llanellen, it was a revelation to see the walls of his living room lined with books. I had only seen that many books in Smith's and in Canon Davies's study at the Vicarage.

So it would be fair to say that my parents, like the rest of the shopkeepers, didn't read; except in one sense this wouldn't be true. My father took two daily newspapers, *The Daily Sketch* and, when that folded, *The Daily Express*, later to be replaced by *The Daily Mail*, together with *The South Wales Argus* in the evening. Then there was the *Abergavenny Chronicle* and *The Radio Times*, as well as other weeklies such as *Picture Post*, *Everybody's*, *Titbits* and my mother's *Woman's Own*. My father, especially, spent a good deal of his time reading. He was an early riser and expected his morning paper to be delivered early so that he could read it over breakfast. Later, when I was also a reader, the *Express* or the *Mail* would be parcelled out between my father and us boys at dinner, a double spread folded and propped against the pepper pot or salt cellar, with conversation limited to 'Have you finished with the middle section yet?' My mother read at table, too; though in general, despite her superior High School education ('Your mother's the clever one in the family,' my father would say) she was less of a committed reader than he was. Later in life, when I sat down to read a book she would start humming a tune or drum her fingers on the arm of her chair. It was as if reading was a challenge she couldn't pass by, as if the book was an affront, both because I had decided to read instead of chatting to her, and because the book cut her out by leading me into an imaginative world where she knew she would never follow. So instead of getting on with something herself, she would sit and hum, ever so innocently, making her presence known, reeling me in. I would try to ignore it but my concentration was broken and I seethed inside, hating her sometimes, because I knew that if confronted with what she was doing, she would deny it and come over all hurt. I never could decide how well she knew herself or her own motives, and that gave her a powerful weapon to use on us boys.

10

What did the shopocracy think, and how did they think? In general they thought in stories. Some people learn to think abstractly by themselves, but on the whole this is rare. Nearly all the shopkeepers of my father's generation had left school at fifteen, and not a few like my father at thirteen. This left him with a good grounding in reading and writing and arithmetic. He must have known the Bible well, too, through school and chapel, though by the time I knew him he seems to have sloughed that off. He had a hazy sense of geography beyond mainland Britain, and a hazier one of history. He never read a poem or a novel in his long life; never owned a record player or went to a concert, though he and my mother half-listened to the dance music of Henry Hall or Victor Sylvester on the radio; he never went to an art gallery. He did see films in his early youth when the cinema was a curiosity (he remembered a travelling show during the First World War with silent films projected in a tent in the Fair Field, and he recalled Tom Mix and Fatty Arbuckle with pleasure), but he never, so far as I know, went to performances at The Pavilion or The Coliseum, the two cinemas in town, built sometime in the 1920s. The discoveries of science passed him by. If he saw a modern painting (usually reproduced in the *Express* or the *Mail*) he would be predictably disgusted. 'Call that art.' Charlie Parker, Thelonius Monk – 'I don't know how you can listen to that racket.' Modern art of any kind was an imposition, a con trick, and with the help of the *Express* and the *Mail,* he wasn't about to be conned. In this he was typical of his shopkeeping acquaintances in the Con Club almost all of whom would have agreed, had they thought about it, that 'the arts' are irrelevant to real life and a scandalous burden on the taxpayer, that is, themselves.

It was stories that defined my father's and my mother's lives, stories that stood in for history, for politics, for literature; stories that could be pulled out in conversation and used as example and counter-example in the shopocracy's version of debate. If politics came up (though this was only ever in private – 'politics and business don't mix'), Labour's iniquities would be enumerated through stories: of known 'dole scroungers' in the town; of Councillor So-and-So's outrageous 'expenses'; of the arch-ogre of the shopocracy, Nye Bevan, coming to the hustings in the Butter Market with charabanc-loads of miners to shout down the Conservatives. When Bevan called the Conservatives 'vermin' sometime in the late 1940s, a badge consisting of a little blue grasshopper with a chirpy face was distributed at the Con Club. It had 'Vermin' written across its body, though I doubt that was the kind of vermin Bevan had in mind. My father wore it in his lapel for a while; the only time I remember him displaying his political allegiance in public. The shopkeepers hated Bevan, the revolutionary who could whip the workers into a frenzy at rallies, whose party planned to take from them everything they had worked so hard for, who would 'ruin the country'.

The stories of the shopocracy were of a particular kind. Folk stories had long since passed out of currency, but the urge to tell stories about their own lives remained, as did the urge to give these a form that was aesthetically pleasing. Despite themselves, art sneaked in at the back door and expressed itself through their own mouths. Because of this, the stories the shopkeepers told had an ambiguous status. They were always based on things that had happened to themselves or to people they knew, and they were therefore considered to be 'true'. At the same time, once an incident established itself as significant enough to be the subject of a story, it was rapidly given a fixed form, so events would always be recounted in the same order, in the same words. It was rare for anything to be added or subtracted in the light of further knowledge about what had really happened. The form of a story, once established, was the truth, and that was that.

Considered as truth, though, these stories were frequently problematic since details that were inconvenient in aesthetic terms were often omitted, while others were embellished or added. As a small child I heard such stories time and again as the grown-ups carried on conversations above my head. I might have been playing with toy soldiers on the floor, but I was listening, too, absorbing the stories into a patchwork quilt of 'things that really happened'. 'Then there was the time we were out on manouevres and had to camouflage our helmets to crawl through a field. I'd put clover in mine but we were told to crawl through a field of ripe wheat. "Barnie," the sergeant said when we reached the hedge, "if I'd been a German you'd be bloody dead by now!"' And my father would give a hoarse chuckle, expelling air between his teeth.

As a child I believed these stories implicitly. When I grew old enough to have been an observer or participant in some of the events that were a story's raw material, though, I became aware of discrepancies. 'No, it didn't happen like that,' I would say to my mother who was the main storyteller in our family, 'So-and-So wasn't there.' Or 'It wasn't at Barry, it was at Porthcawl.' Sometimes she would disagree but more often she would say 'Oh yes, that's right.' Next time she told the tale, however, the discrepancy between what I knew had happened and the story of what happened would still be there. I used to think she had forgotten and I would correct her again. Only now, thinking about it long after they are dead, have I come to realise that, my mother especially, had a conditional sense of the truth. Detail was important to the story version of an event, but not all the detail, and if it didn't happen at Barry like she said, or if So-and-So had been somewhere else at the time, it didn't matter so long as it didn't interfere with the event-as-story, the refined version which she would always tell in the same way with utter conviction until the day she died.

This used to annoy me because I had quite a good memory and because it seemed to me that the truth of an event should be respected. A Postmodernist would no doubt say that one version of an event is as 'true' as another, but that is an evasion which fails to take into account the possibility of finding out what happened through analysis, through comparison with sources that are independent of the storyteller, where they exist. In many cases of course that is not possible because the evidence hasn't survived; it doesn't mean there is no definitive truth, merely that in this instance we are unable to arrive at it. My mother was far more prone to the story-as-truth than my father who often sat back while she told his stories. 'Tell them the one about the time you broke your wrist in the Blitz, Ted.' 'No, you tell it.' 'Well . . .' At times, though, even he noticed how she distorted events for artistic purposes. 'No,' he would say, warming his legs at the fire, 'that's not how it happened.'

She never tired of telling the same story over and over, having apparently forgotten that she told it you last week, and many times in the months and years before that. She would always do so with great enthusiasm, sure that it was new. Somehow it was impossible to interrupt and say that you'd heard it. Sometimes my father would, though, aware perhaps that you were as bored as he was – 'Oh you've told them that one.' And then she would break off and seem hurt. For her, the stories had become a substitute world, freshly painted every time she told them, but it was a world that removed her by infinitely small degrees from things as they are.

11

After I entered Sixth Form, my education took me on a collision course with this way of relating to the world. I was beginning to encounter ideas about politics and religion, and to question assumptions that were unquestioned and unquestionable in the world of the shopocracy. I became vehemently anti-Christian and felt resentment at the way I had been forced to go to church as a child, culminating in my confirmation, even though I had never ever believed any of Christianity's doctrines or myths.

Both my parents had strict Edwardian upbringings in which Christianity and church or chapel attendance were central. As children, each had gone to morning and evening service on a Sunday and attended Sunday school in the afternoon. There would have been a strong emphasis on obedience. I still have the *Certificate of Merit* 'Presented to Melva Fletcher for attendance and conduct at Christ Church Sunday School in 1919' when she was eleven, signed by Canon Davies, Vicar of St Mary's, who thirty-seven years later would preside over my own unwilling confirmation.

Yet my parents, and the shopocracy in general, were the generation that broke with Christianity in its formal manifestation. When I knew them, neither my mother nor my father went to church even at Christmas or Easter. They would have a lie-in, meaning in my father's case getting up at seven instead of six, then my mother would start preparing the Sunday roast, the climax of the week's cooking, or if it was summer and fine weather, the car would be loaded with picnic paraphernalia and we would be off down the empty Hereford Road, past St Mary's Church, standing grey and silent between early morning and morning services.

In winter, though, they expected me to go, and at ten in the morning I would have to put on my short-trousered grey suit, grey shirt and a tie, grey socks held up below the knees with elastic, my shoes shinily black, polished by my mother. At half-past, Mrs Simpson would call in at the back door, and with the bells of St Mary's peeling over and over – dee-dee-dee-dee-dah-dah-dah-dum; dee-dee-dee-dee-dah-dah-dah-dum; dee-dee-dee-dee-dah-dah-dah-dum – I would walk with her down Hereford Road, joining the trickle of worshippers, mostly old women, on their way to St Mary's. I called Mrs Simpson 'aunt'; she and her husband and their son Colin had been billeted on us during the War. They had the front room and the two bedrooms on the second floor; the bathroom and kitchen had to be shared. Mr Simpson was Station Master at the LMS junction out on the Ross Road, and after the War they moved to Ross House at the end of Priory Road, a hundred yards from us, which was overlooked by Pen-y-fal Asylum with its shady rook-filled trees across the Gavenny where you could see the mentally ill – prisoners, as I used to think of them – walking aimlessly in their high-walled exercise yard, or sitting and staring, or shouting angrily and tearing their hair.

From the beginning I resented church-going and began to form arguments. 'Why should I go if you don't go?' 'Because . . .' 'If you don't go to church you can't be Christians.' 'Yes we can.' 'Then why don't you go?' 'Because we've been working hard in the shop all week and your Dad and I need a rest.' 'Then why should I go?'

My parents were uneasy with this kind of probing which would end in my mother saying 'Because I say so' or 'We went when we were little', and Mrs Simpson would put her head round the back door and I would slouch out to meet her. The services were appallingly boring and it was the boredom I resented most; that sense of dread as we crossed the doorstep of the church out of the sun and into the shadow, the purple baize doors whispering shut behind us, the organ rumbling with little reedy glissandos as if the organist was bored too and couldn't be bothered with more than doodles. 'Let us pray', and the congregation of forty or fifty manoeuvered stiff knees down onto hassocks with an occasional discreet echoing cough, sucking mints during the sermon, the Vicar looking down on us from the pulpit like an intelligent rook.

To emerge from the church's shadow into sunlight was to return to reality, the Black Mountains bright on the horizon, daffodils shining and bouncing in the park as we walked past. As soon as I got in the house I went upstairs and threw off the stiff suit, the tie, the ugly black shoes and went down to dinner, the kitchen windows dripping with condensation, *Forces' Favourites* on the radio, the smell of roasting lamb – and was myself again.

Resistance to Christianity was the beginning of a revolt against my parents and the shopocracy, done in the crude and sometimes brutal way of teenagers. After my confirmation (the dedication in the *Book of Common Prayer* says this was on the 10th of May, 1956), I rarely went to St Mary's. When I did it was to make a point. I went once with my friend Roynon, whose father was a police inspector, a church warden and a big man in the choir; we'd dressed in our ordinary clothes, without ties, and refused to stand when the Vicar, at the head of the choir, processed down the aisle at the start of the service. Mrs Simpson was in the congregation and must have reported back, leading to a row with my parents. But even as Roynon and I did it, we knew it was a meaningless gesture and it was never repeated. Instead I took the fight against Christianty into the house, asking my parents what they thought about free will, the virgin birth, the nature of miracles, transubstantiation, and the resurrection. These were issues a small group of us at the Grammar School discussed endlessly, making appointments at one time to see clergymen from the various denominations, asking Canon Davies what he thought about free will in his book-lined study in the big Victorian vicarage on the Hereford Road, and getting the Catholic priest to give an opinion on transubstantiation. Little Protestants that we were, we were less than impressed when the priest took down a black-covered book from a shelf behind him to read out the Church's official teaching. Why couldn't he think for himself?

The problem, as regards the collision course with my parents, was that no one in the shopocracy thought about religion – any more than they thought about Conservatism – as a set of propositions that could be considered and accepted or rejected. They had almost to a man and woman turned their backs on religion as a living force which involved acts of worship on their part; there were no particular articles of faith which they believed in. Yet they hadn't made a conscious decision to reject Christianity either. They were not agnostic. If pressed, they would say 'Of course we're Christians', whereas really they were secularists, the first generation to exploit and enjoy the proliferating inventions and material comfort afforded by twentieth-century technology. Yet because of their intensely religious upbringing, Christianity was part of their shadow, which they couldn't jump across; it was always there, grey and half-remembered, a force not for salvation of the soul, but the perpetuation of decency and respectability. Its function was social. Agnostic was a word they probably had never heard of, but they knew what an atheist was, it was a rebel, someone who kicked against the traces, who was outside the bounds of decent society through denying one of its core beliefs – that respectability equalled 'Christianity', even though by the time I knew them they only had a hazy idea of what Christianity was. At a time when issues like free will versus predestination were a topic of intense discussion between me and my friends, the hypocrisy (as I saw it) of my parents' position on religion used to make me angry. I was too close to understand that this was unintentional on their part; that they were a product of the twentieth century's great contest between Christianity and materialism in which, for most of the century, materialism appeared to be winning out.

But rejecting their world didn't mean that I became entirely free of it, any more than my parents were freed from the world of their parents, trailing the tatters of Christianity behind them as they embraced twentieth-century secularism. Notions of respectability lie deep in some of my attitudes, and though I am an atheist, I hesitate to use the word about myself; it still retains an aura of the disreputable, of the boundary-crosser who rejects society, like a character out of Dostoyevsky. Nor have I and some of my Abergavenny friends escaped Christianity in that it is still a cause of anger; a set of bony delusions we have to gnaw on again and again.

Just as it was mostly older women who made up the sparse congregations at St Mary's in the 1950s, so it was my mother who was the most insistent that I become confirmed, because if I didn't it would be a mark against her; evidence that she hadn't brought me up properly. My father, on the other hand, perhaps because he was from a chapel background, was more indifferent, just as he was more speculative about religion. Somewhere or other he had come across the idea of the transmigration of souls and had a lot of fun imagining what he might return as. After he retired, he attended services at the Congregational chapel for a while, but gave it up because he kept falling asleep during the sermon. More than my mother, too, there was an element in him which actively questioned Christianity. Sitting by the kitchen fire one day he asked what kind of god it was who could sacrifice his only son in that terrible way on the cross, and I knew he was thinking about himself and us boys, and about giving us up of his own free will to be tortured and humiliated, and to die in agony. He knew he could never do that, and if he, a mere human, couldn't, what did god's decision say about him; in what way was he a god of love? I respected him for that. I think he was wrong about my mother being the clever one.

As they lay dying, neither of my parents turned to religion for comfort. They were both given Christian burials, my father with a certain ambiguity from Ted Williams's Chapel of Rest just round the corner from the Conservative Club. Sitting in the chief mourners' car on the way to the crematorium at Croesyceiliog, I could see Mr Williams and one of his assistants through the rear window of the hearse in front. Top-hatted, they preserved a funereal speed to the edge of town, then Mr Williams removed the hat and put his foot down; I could see him chatting, relaxed, a hand raised now and then to make a point. A jovial associate of the shopocracy himself, 'Not Ted Barnie!' he had said over the phone when I asked him to undertake the funeral. He had come to the house with a shallow black lacquered coffin to collect the corpse and take it to the Chapel of Rest, everything respectful and efficient.

My mother's funeral took place at St Mary's, the vicar, who had never met her, coming to the house to gather information about her life for the funeral address.

12

In many ways the shopkeepers were exemplars of the twentieth century's Modern Man. They were not technophobes and embraced technological advance eagerly. My father was a car owner by the mid 1920s. In the days before driving tests and licences, the garage owner showed him how to operate the gears and the brake, and off he went like Mr Toad in the direction of Monmouth. Unfortunately the instructions hadn't included 'reverse' and my father had to drive down the narrow road until he found a place where he could turn in a full circle in order to get back to Abergavenny. One of his vehicles was an Overland Whippet which was a convertible. The bodywork of the car could be lifted off with a block and tackle in our garage and replaced with the superstructure of a van which was then bolted to the chassis. This was handy at a time when he was trying to develop his business as a wholesaler to corner shops in the Valleys.

The first car I remember was a black Standard 13. It had running boards and doors that opened forwards; the opposite of car doors today which are no doubt safer but less easy to get in and out of. Whenever he came to a downward slope on a hill, my father would switch off the engine and the car would gather speed under the force of gravity, the hedges whipping past, the slipstream whistling as it snagged on some part of the bodywork. The best was the mile or more glide from Bwlch, halfway between Brecon and Crickhowell. After we reached the top of the ridge and the bonnet of the Standard 13 pointed down, everybody became silent and we began a headlong glide, my mother and father sitting smoking in the front, we boys leaning forward willing the car on and on as it entered the flat. Eventually, as the car came almost to a standstill, my father would reluctantly switch the engine back on and the journey would be normal again. After Bwlch there were no more good slopes.

My father did this to save petrol, he said, but I suspect that like us boys he found it exciting as well. I had just caught the end of the heroic age of the car, before road widening which destroyed the old roads around Abergavenny, before the Heads of the Valleys gashed its way past Llanfoist, Govilon and Gilwern, and you couldn't escape the monotonous drone and grind of traffic anywhere in our part of the Usk Valley.

There were the tales too. When I worked as a bus conductor on the Western Welsh before going to university, one of the drivers, Trevor Bowen, told me how in summer, if he was driving a charter bus with day-trippers, he would slide open the long sun roof and passengers would climb up and sit outside, their legs dangling down into the interior. This would have been in the 1930s, Trevor's high times as a young driver.

Even by the 1930s, though, the warning signs were there to see. My father drove to London once. 'Never again.' He had gone round and round Picadilly Circus trying to find the exit he wanted in the aggressive scramble of traffic, until eventually a policeman standing on traffic duty in the middle started to salute him. The roads of rural Monmouthshire might still be undeveloped, the streets of the towns and villages leisurely and quiet (eerily so by modern standards), but the car, which he and his kind took to so easily, was about to destroy it all. My father was part of the dilemma of a prosperous mass society in a way that he, like many others, never understood or came to terms with. Car ownership was an evident good which is why he bought one, but when car ownership spread, it became less good, crowding the towns, leading to 'road improvements', by-passes, motorways, streets crowded with parked cars in front of houses built without garages. The balance between the quiet small-town world he had grown up with and was at home in, and the process of modernisation which he had quickly embraced, became more difficult to maintain until toward the end of his life in the 1970s, it was destroyed. He would grumble about this, stuck in traffic at the new lights by the the Vic, the Victoria pub, on the Hereford Road. 'Look at all this traffic – it's ridiculous!'

My aunt and uncle, May and Ernie Hodges, the tobacconists and gents' hairdressers, had lived all their married lives in a big semi-detached Edwardian house just down from the Vic. At the side was a kitchen garden enclosed in a high wall built of Deri sandstone. Ernie, like my father, had been an early car owner, exchanging his old one for a new model every year. This was considered wasteful and pretentious by Don and Ted, his suspicious and perhaps envious brothers-in-law. 'But it pays, Ted, when you consider the depreciation.' 'Perhaps you're right, Ernie.' Ernie's car was kept polished like the Queen's and if it was raining he wouldn't take it out. If it rained while he was out, the car had to be dried off and polished before it was put away. At least that's what was said in the family. The chrome radiator and racing green or black bonnet certainly gleamed in the depths of his garage.

Ernie and May were hovering close to the elite of the shopocracy, their shop being larger and a cut above ours. It had two counters either side as you walked in, the right-hand counter given over to cigarettes and tobacco and shiny polished pipes, the left to handbags and leather goods. A frosted door at the back gave onto the barber's shop, a secret male world where Ernie and two assistants in white coats clipped hair all day, a carpet of curls accumulating at their feet. Naturally, because it was family, I was expected to have my hair cut there too, and had to submit to the rigid procedures of a short-back-and-sides and a deeply incised left-hand parting. When Ernie and May retired a few years before my father, the shop was taken over by their daughter Dorothy and her husband Harold Gwenlan. Harold had been a clerk on the Great Western, working in the ticket office at Abergavenny

Monmouth Road (in the days when the town had three stations). He had married into the shopocracy.

Harold Gwenlan was a quiet and inoffensive man, even if, perhaps, his marriage had given him pretensions in his younger days. Toward the end of his life he was paralysed by a stroke. He could barely talk and was unable to walk, though his 'faculties', as my mother would say, were all there. Dorothy had to drive him everywhere with a collapsible wheelchair in the back of the car. She would park in Priory Road outside our back door and pop in for a quick coffee and a chat. My mother would go out to see Harold who remained in the car, and on the assumption that he was on a par with the few foreigners she'd met, since he could only mumble, she would bend down and talk to him loudly and slowly through the front passenger window. Coming back from town one day, I found him crying to himself and didn't know what to say.

In some ways, May and Ernie died just in time. Their big old house was sold off and turned into offices, while the kitchen garden was compulsorily purchased, its Deri stone wall knocked down by the Council. A swathe of Bailey Park was appropriated too, and a new road created to divert traffic around the town. 'It's a good job May and Ernie aren't here to see this,' one of my parents would say, as we waited at the lights by the Vic, traffic streaming round by the Hodges' old house; traffic queueing in a long line past the Vicarage for the lights to change, backing up behind us on the Hereford Road.

It was the same with television. Like many others, my father bought our first set in time for the Coronation in 1953. Set up in a corner of the 'dining room' (really the lounge, looking onto the back yard; the larger front room was rarely used except at Christmas), the set changed the physical orientation of our lives. Previously the easy chairs had been arranged to face the fireplace; now they faced the television and were never turned away again. On the day of the Coronation, the dining room was crowded with family and neighbours who still didn't have a set, watching the black-and-white processions and fanfares that seemed to go on for hours. We boys soon got bored and went outside to play.

The Coronation was one of the last set pieces of the old imperial order, to which the shopocracy subscribed. When George VI died, I was in my last year in the primary school run by nuns of the Convent of the Sacred Heart. We were at our desks writing quietly, the Sister at the teacher's desk, her face pinched and disembodied from all fleshly thoughts by the stiff, starched head-dress, concealing the slightest wisp of hair, when the Mother Superior came in, whispered to her and then turned round to face us. 'Children, I have some terrible news. T h e K i n g i s d e a d.' We were awed, as much by the the importance the nuns gave to this event as by the event itself, which I don't think meant anything to us. The school was closed and we were sent home. There was nothing on the radio all day except sombre classical music.

In a few years, royalty and Empire would be included among my targets for rebellion. When I was nine or ten, we were given little paper Union Jacks on sticks and the nuns took us down the road to stand near the Monument with its exhausted bronze soldier, who leaned on his upturned rifle, staring at the main street he would never see again. There was an air of expectancy in the crowd and then someone shouted 'Here she comes!' and we all leaned out and waved our flags as a shiny black limousine purred past, taking Princess Margaret to the South Wales Borderers' HQ at Cwrt-y-gollen. I saw the wave of a white hand and glimpsed a face, and then it was over and we went back to school.

When I was seventeen, I walked out of the Pavilion cinema while they were playing 'God Save the Queen', as they did at the end of every evening performance, and as they did after shows at the Town Hall Theatre and even on television before the phosphorous glow of the white dot faded in the middle of the screen. You were supposed to stand to attention; it was like being in church. As I walked up the central aisle of the Pav, a middle-aged man grabbed my arm, but I wrenched it away and walked on. I suppose he was trying to teach me 'manners', but I was listening to Bill Haley and the Comets singing 'See you later, alligator' on a Dansette record player in the front room, and was no longer to be trammelled by that man's world, so I thought.

Television soon replaced radio in my parents' lives and we settled easily into a new routine around a screen that got bigger every time my father bought a new set. In the 1950s, with only one BBC channel and broadcasting limited to a few hours each evening, there was still time to do other things; but as channels proliferated and broadcasting was extended through the evening, television came to fill my parents' lives. By the mid 1960s the set would be on from the *Six O'Clock News* until close down.

All the soaps were watched and the family began the process whereby the characters in *Coronation Street* or *Emmerdale Farm* became a parallel community to the one we lived in. In the case of *Coronation Street* my parents would have watched a couple of fictional generations grow up and grow old. My father still went to the club and my mother met Mrs Shackleton and Dorothy for a coffee evening once a week, but otherwise the evenings were spent in front of the television set. After he retired, my father enjoyed broadcasts of horse racing in the afternoons, and fixed up an account with his bookmaker so that he could phone in bets while he watched. He also never missed snooker tournaments. My mother loved Wimbledon and the soaps, and the memorial service on Armistice Day. They would sit and smoke, drink Nescafé and doze, my father waking now and then to switch channels and grumble that there was 'nothing on'. The set would nonetheless never be switched off. Even when a neighbour or a member of the family called, it would be left on with the sound turned down, everyone's eyes glancing now and then in its direction. As they grew old, channels proliferated beyond any need or meaning until, like the car, television impoverished rather than enriched their lives.

13

Sex was a word the shopocracy never used. Had they compiled a dictionary, there would have been no entry under *sex*. So when it invaded my life when I was fourteen I had no idea what was happening; it was as if my body had decided to take on a powerful and uncontrollable existence of its own. The same thing must have happened to my father and the other shopkeepers. Looking at the photographs of my grandfather, it is inconceivable that John Henderson would have taken his sons aside one by one and told them about 'the facts of life'. When, as an eighteen-year-old, my cousin Geoffrey went to join the Merchant Navy in Newport in 1944, his father, my Uncle Don, walked part of the way with him from the Mardy to the station and warned him about prostitutes; but that was the nearest anyone got to sex education that I heard of.

The men must have thought about sex and been driven by sex like males of any generation, but looking back, there are only the slightest of hints. One reason for taking the aptly named *Titbits* must have been because of the sweater girls who grinned at you mockingly as they pushed out their breasts. Then there was *The News of the World* which gave graphic accounts (though not by today's standards) of divorce cases as they unfolded in court. 'The defendant, council for the prosecution claimed, had been seen entering the Albemarle Hotel with Miss ——, a prostitute well known to the police, on the evening of 24th March where he was registered under the name of Smith . . .'

When my newly married parents moved into Elmsgrove, our house on the Hereford Road, they had found a pile of 1930s pornography stashed up the flue of the fireplace in one of the second-storey bedrooms, so they told me later. It would have been destroyed; it was nothing to do with them.

In the boys-only grammar school, sex was only discussed in a vague way by some of the older boys, one of whom had claimed to have done it with D—— on the hard wooden benches of the Pavilion in Bailey Park. We younger boys were impressed with this but secretly doubted it could be true. Girls, it was generally agreed, didn't like sex. I studied Human Biology for O-level and the Biology mistress (the only woman in the school apart from the secretary) told us that for women it hurt. We weren't sure whether we believed this or not, but on balance most of us probably did. Diagrams she drew of the male and female reproductive organs were about as sexless as it was possible to get, a perfectly limp penis in white chalk staring down at us for the forty minutes of the lesson.

When as a small boy I caught my mother and father embracing in the scullery as he came in from the shop for dinner, and even worse, kissing, I was shocked. They never did that; they almost never touched each other.

Once every few weeks my mother would come downstairs in the morning and place a bundle discreetly on the back of the coal fire in the kitchen. Nothing was ever said but somehow I knew it was something I should never ask about.

Early in the War the manager of the Coliseum, who lived near us down Priory Road, was arrested by the police. He was at the centre of what would now be called a paedophile ring at the cinema and my parents could read about it in *The News of the World*. Even more ignorant about these things than Queen Victoria, my mother didn't know what a homosexual was, and since there was no dictionary in the house, she had to ask my father. It's hard to imagine what he told her. The manager killed himself.

My father would have been in his mid-thirties when he courted my mother. He was a successful shopkeeper and in his

Martha Barnie,
Ted Barnie's
mother, wrapped
up for the beach.
Late 1930s.

Ted Barnie, c. 1933.

Melva Barnie and John Barnie aged 2½, 1943, taken at Shackleton's studio.

John Barnie sweeping leaves at Norman Place, c. 1944.

In the countryside, c. 1950.

Michael and John Barnie, c. 1950.

John Barnie, c. 1951.

John and Melva paddling, South Wales, c. 1950.

A day at the seaside. Left to right: Marjorie Wilcock, Ted Barnie, Bert Wilcock, John Barnie, Lil Wilcock, in front, Michael Barnie, c. 1950.

Sailing model boats, the ornamental gardens, Bournmouth, c. 1952.

On the putting green.

Ted Barnie in the shop with Nancy Legge (centre) and Melva Barnie, c. 1955-60.

John, Michael, Melva and Ted, Bournemouth, c. 1950.

small way a man about town; she was in her late twenties, working in Clarke's shoe shop. She still lived with her uncle and aunt in North Street who had helped bring her up, and Uncle Fred insisted that she had to be in by 10pm. When my father's car broke down one evening and they were late, Uncle Fred didn't believe him and he gave my father a row at the door.

Sunday afternoons, if we weren't planning an outing, my mother and father would go upstairs for a nap while my brother and I played in the dining room, or on the back lawn if it was summer. Out on the lawn I would glance up from time to time at their bedroom window, wondering how long they would be, the bottom half of the window wedged open with a stick because the sash cord had gone. The top pane was grey or blue, reflecting the sky; the open half opaque and dark and silent. Sometime in the late 1950s my parents exchanged the double bed for two singles and a bedside table.

When I started listening to the blues as a sixteen-year-old, I discovered an exuberant, unselfconscious celebration of sex, but there were no Big-Butter-and-Egg-Men making the bedsprings whine among the shopkeepers, so far as I ever knew. Whatever their sex lives were, the shopocracy took the secret with them to the grave.

14

The shopkeepers of my father's generation in Abergavenny were lucky with the Second World War. Most were too old for active service, some having fought as long ago as the Boer War and others, like my father's brother Don, in the First World War, while their children, for the most part, were still too young; though there were exceptions. A cousin on the Monmouth side of the family was killed in Italy and another badly wounded at Arnhem. I only met the Arnhem survivor once or twice and the connection seemed to me as a child very distant. He went into the book trade, working for Blackwells in Oxford. For the rest, it was at worst the Home Guard or fire duty. Two bombs fell in a field at Bryn-y-gwenin, straddling a farm and killing some chickens, and a Spitfire crashed into the Big Skirrid, killing the pilot. At night you could hear the thrum-thrum-thrum of the German bombers' engines as they past overhead on their way to Liverpool and see the searchlights snap on all up the Usk valley, following their flight path with stiff beams of light. And there was rationing, including sweets, so that the small and irregular deliveries had to be doled out with care, regular customers getting preference.

My father, who was thirty-seven when war broke out, was given several deferments because of the shop and because by the summer of 1940 his wife was pregnant with me, her first child. As the situation worsened, however, he was drafted and told by the Ministry of War either to find some other means of keeping the shop open or to close it down. This must have been in late 1942 or early 1943 when I was eighteen months or two years old. Since the shop was the only source of income, my mother took it over, and her aunt, my great-aunt, May Wood, looked after me. My mother would wheel me in the pram up to the tiny nineteenth-century cottage in North Street, grandly named Norman Place, and there I would stay until I was collected after closing time. In this way my Aunt May became a surrogate mother to me and I was very close to her. Norman Place became a second home and remained so long after the war ended.

When it did, I was four, and I suppose it was only then that I began to know my father. I have one clear memory of him on leave; the rough texture of his khaki uniform, and his rifle, propped against a wall in the kitchen. It was taller than me and too heavy to lift. I think that is the only real memory. The rest are secondary memories based on my parents' stories, told so early and so often that I feel they are mine, like the one about how I shouted 'Daddy! Daddy!' from my pram every time I saw a soldier in uniform, to my mother's embarrassment.

It would have been hard for them, my mother with a new baby and a shop to run, my father in early middle age plunged into basic training with recruits who were generally in their late teens. He was a gentle man who never raised his voice or physically punished either of us boys, and he must have hated it for the alien harshness of it all as much as for the danger to come. He would have made a poor front-line soldier and his lack of potential was recognised because, in the build-up to the Normandy invasion, he was assigned to an auxiliary unit whose role was to supply the assault troops after a bridgehead had been established. So he was trained to drive 5-ton covered lorries, manoeuvres including learning how to drive in convoy at night with the lorry's lights reduced to the narrowest of slits. Even keeping close to the lorry in front, it was easy to topple over into a ditch.

His unit was deployed to London where he was detailed to the docks, loading ships in preparation for the invasion. It must have been the time of the V1 and V2 rockets because he remembered whole rows of houses that had been standing when he passed in the morning reduced to rubble by the time he returned at night.

One evening some of the unit asked him if he'd like to go to the cinema, but he was too tired. The cinema took a direct hit and everyone was killed. As you worked, you could hear the motor of the V1's puttering overhead. When it stopped, you held your breath.

One day, high on a stack of packing cases at the dockside, he stepped back into thin air and fell, breaking his wrist very badly. This must have been on the eve of the invasion because he was transferred to Cardiff Royal Infirmary to be treated and there he saw some of the most awful sights he had ever seen as the wounded were brought in from the initial landings. Men with no legs, blind men, men bandaged from head to foot with burns; one man with a broken back, held screaming between two chairs while nurses wound a plaster-of-Paris bandage round him. He never forgot this and nor did my mother who went there to visit him, but his wrist was not set properly so he only had limited movement in it for the rest of his life, and for him the war was over, his experience soon assimilated into the fund of familiar stories that defined my parents' lives, to be told and retold with a chuckle, or, looking into the fire, 'Aye, poor devils, some of them had it bad.'

The shopocracy had only a vague sense of a narrative history of the Second World War which was derived entirely from radio news bulletins and newspaper reports of the time and was therefore piecemeal and patriotic. They had little understanding of the causes of the war or of events on the Eastern Front. Churchill was the great war leader, the man of destiny, and my parents would tell how they listened to his broadcasts to the nation and were inspired. They knew that America had played a part and that without the Lend-Lease scheme Britain would not have been able to continue the war after 1941, but for them it was a British war. It was us against Hitler. I don't think they ever appreciated the scale of American involvement in the Normandy landings and never understood the crucial importance of the Eastern Front and the awfulness of the sacrifices of the Russian people. By the late 1940s they were already drawn mentally and imaginatively into the Cold War where communist Russia was the enemy and the deciding role of the USSR in the war was forgotten. Once the war ended, their knowledge of it came to a standstill. Because they never read books, they never read a history of the most momentous upheaval of the twentieth century which they had lived through; they were content to recall their own peripheral experience of it in the form of well-crafted stories, and with sentiments like, 'What they did to the Jews was awful.' Were they alive now, they could have been interviewed for a modish 'people's history' of the war, a book they might even have read, or at least leafed through to look at the illustrations. 'Oh I remember that.'

In a way that I find hard to explain, the Second World War cast a longer shadow over me than it did over my parents who by the early 1950s were getting on with their small-town lives. By the middle of that decade, veterans of the war were beginning to publish their memoirs, and I bought these at Smith's with my pocket money. *The Colditz Story*, *The Dam Busters*, Douglas Bader's *Reach for the Sky* were all read eagerly by me, though I doubt my parents even bothered to look at the blurb on the dust cover. Colin Simpson, who was several years older than me and had been in the ATC, gave me a Second World War practice morse-tapper which I still have. Black and utility-heavy and ugly, it was the most beautiful thing in the world when I was twelve. You depressed the bakelite ball of the handle and you could hear the lengths of the sounds the machine was making – dippitydee dippitydeedeedee – just like the ships you could hear at night on short-wave radio, talking to each other out in the Atlantic. Or that's where I imagined them to be. Although I got a copy of the morse code and practised with it, I was never good enough to follow the rapid conversations of the cargo ships or trawlers in the mysterious ocean far beyond the hills of Monmouthshire.

I acquired other war relics. A black, metal-cased hand compass with a lid that flipped up and had a mirror on the inside. A white arrow pointed through an arch cut out of the base of the mirror and the circular compass could be turned on the metal base. The lid shut with a satisfying military click. I was told, or persuaded myself, that it was an RAF compass. Only many years later did it dawn on me that because instead of an E for East there was an O (for Ost) this was in fact a German compass, perhaps part of a Luftwaffe survival kit, carried by aircrew in case they were shot down over enemy territory. It may have been found in a wreck or acquired from a prisoner of war.

I also had a set of photographs, like a pack of cards, showing grainy images of British, American, German and Japanese fighters and bombers, taken at characteristic angles which made them easy to identify. They were used to train aircrew and spotters assigned to anti-aircraft batteries in aircraft recognition. I became an expert, or so I liked to think, at distinguishing a Spitfire from a Hurricane, a Messerschmitt ME 109 from a Focke-Wulf FW 190, flinging the cards down at random on the table and shouting out their names before checking on the back to see if I had got it right.

Then there are the stories in which I was involved, though I can no longer decide if these are true memories or stories told so often by my mother that I have re-imagined them and internalised them as my own. There is the one about the desert-camouflaged convoy stretching the whole length of the Hereford Road and how as a three-year-old, I rushed into the front room which was Mr and Mrs Simpson's sitting room and stood on Mr Simpson's bowler hat to get a better view. Or the one about a day trip to Porthcawl. My father must have had a few days' leave and we had gone there by train as there was no petrol for cars. Walking down a sandy concrete ramp to the beach, a tall black American soldier smiled at me, reached down, and gave me a stick of chewing gum which was retrieved by my parents as I was too young to eat it. I will never know if I really remember that.

By the mid 1950s, too, I was going to the cinema to see the

stream of black-and-white war films that had begun to appear, patriotic and self-glorifying, about Dunkirk, escape from Stalag Luft II, the Battle of Britain, the Desert Rats, the destruction of the *Tirpitz*, in which it was us against the Nazis, with rarely an American and never a Russian in sight. This was heroic war that turned defeat into victory, where the heroes were always English officers who played with a straight bat.

As an undergraduate, though, I began reading different books – Alan Bullock's *Hitler, A Study in Tyranny*, Erwin Leiser's *A Pictorial History of Nazi Germany*, Hugh Trevor-Roper's *The Last Days of Hitler*, and there were the television documentaries, about the concentration camps, the war at sea, the war in the Far East, a world of grey faces, endless columns of tanks, the flash-flash-flash of artillery barrages, a world of endurance and terrible suffering and cruelty. Gradually over time, the war came to influence my ideas on humanity, on what we are as a species; on our capabilities – and our limitations.

The war and its aftermath affected my parents differently. Like most of the shopocracy, they had been on its fringes. It had been terrible, yes, but it was over, and they returned to the daily routine of the shops and small-town life. Now and again they would recall incidents from experience, but transformed into 'Tales of What Happened in the War' that were added to the storehouse of oral literature by means of which they narrated the world.

'It's a pity about poor Don,' my mother would remark apropos of nothing, about my cousin who died in Italy. 'He was a sergeant, you know, and very well liked by his men.'

15

Because, for the most part, the shopkeepers and their wives came from poor or at best modest backgrounds, they always tended to be what they would call 'careful'. This took many forms. One was a cautious attitude to business. My father's ice cream was so popular that he was urged several times to expand and set up a small factory, selling to cafés in south-east Wales. He pretended to consider this but never did anything about it. There is a dividing line between being a shopkeeper and being an entrepreneur and my father's generation never crossed it. Those who inherited a shop from *their* fathers made few changes. Dorothy and Harold ran the tobacconists and gents' hairdressers in much the same way that Ernie and May had done. When my father retired in 1969, Dorothy had the idea of taking over his business as a going concern. It was next door and her family had always owned the premises. But each business has its own terms of reference, and the skills and experience needed to run a sweet shop are different from those needed to run a tobacconist's. The sweet shop didn't prosper and, after a year or so, Dorothy and Harold reverted to renting it out.

Mr Shackleton had inherited the chemist's from his father who had founded it. He made few changes, apart from abandoning the photographic studio which had been an interest of his father's. Here for many years townspeople went to have their children photographed, or to have a formal engagement photo taken. The studio was entered through a narrow alleyway at the side of the shop and there, during the war years, I was taken for a portrait with my mother. Although, like many chemists, Bill Shackleton kept on the camera and film side of the business, he was content to stay in the dispensary himself. Only when his son took over did Shackleton's expand, at first by taking over another chemist's in town and then establishing a small chain.

This kind of entrepreneurialism was beyond the shopkeepers of my father's generation. They did not aspire to it. Having come up from nothing, they were content to hold on to their businesses, which gave them a reasonable living. They were by nature savers. Mindful of his old age, my father made steady and cautious investments in stocks and shares, always investing in government bonds or blue chip companies. He never speculated by buying and selling then rebuying when prices fell; that would have been too risky, and the shopkeepers avoided risk. His aim was to build up a retirement fund, a kind of self-made pension, and in this he was successful.

Carefulness in large things was mirrored by carefulness in small things. When my father emptied a bottle of milk into the milk jug, he would balance the empty bottle carefully at an angle against the jug's rim and leave it there for several minutes so that every last drop of milk would be drained out of it. For years when we were children, my brother and I would have our bath after my father, using his bath water. Bath night was Sunday night and nobody ever had a bath more than once a week. The bath was a large, deep Edwardian one on cast-iron lion-claw legs; it must have been there since the house was built in about 1903. My father liked to fill the bath almost to the rim and to lie and soak before washing. Then it was the turn of us boys, cocking a leg over the high rim to sink up to the shoulders in tepid water that was a pale soapy grey, with a line of grime beginning to form around the bath at water level. No doubt this is how it had been at the Old Gaol in Monmouth with seven children as well as two adults queuing for their weekly bath. To my father it made sense; the water was there, it was still warm, why waste it? To us boys, it was simply things as they are.

It was the same with fires. Although there was a fireplace in every room in the house, including the bedrooms, in winter a fire was only ever lit in one room at a time. In the morning this would be the kitchen, my father laying and lighting it as soon as he got up. It would be banked with nutty slack during the day and with luck would still be in when we got home, the hard crust of slack cracked open with the poker to reveal a tired red eye of glowing coal. At 6 o'clock the fire would be lit in the dining room and the one in the kitchen allowed to go out. We would all move from room to room, following the warmth. Lights too would be turned on and off, following our progress. My father came from a world where nothing was wasted. 'The only thing you can't eat on a pig,' he used to say, 'is its whistle.' This must have been reinforced in the war years when rationing made everything scarce; being 'careful', ingrained in his generation from childhood, was a useful discipline then.

And they were all like that. May Hodges, my father's eldest sister, would come in from the tobacconist's and while talking to my father would edge round the counter. Bending at right angles from the waist (something all women of her generation did) she picked up pieces of string that had been ripped quickly off sweet boxes when the shop was busy. These she tied into a single length and wound round her fingers. When she left ten minutes later, she had a ball of string to be used next door. In her old age, after Ernie had died, these traits were exaggerated into what can only be called eccentricity. She had a gas stove in the kitchen in perfect working order, but never used it. Instead she cooked on a primus stove on the kitchen floor with, it may be, four saucepans balanced one on top of the other, one with meat, one with carrots, one with potatoes and one with gravy, all bubbling and steaming away. If you happened to call while she was cooking, she would take you into the kitchen to admire it, hands folded in front of her, with a cat-like satisfaction. I almost expected her to purr. In the living room she had a gas fire. Half the holes for the gas jet were blocked off, stuffed with paper. This was clearly dangerous and was talked about in the family, my father expressing the view that May was taking things too far. At Norman Place in North Street, my great aunt and uncle's house where I spent so much time as a child, the only toilet was in an outhouse divided between the toilet and the coal shed. Instead of toilet paper, my aunt cut newspaper into hand-sized squares, bored a hole through them at one corner and threaded them together with string. These were hung on a hook on the back of the toilet door and you ripped the sheets off one by one. I don't think they took a newspaper, so they must have got old copies from a neighbour, perhaps, or my parents.

In the 1940s and 1950s refuse bins were known as dustbins because each week when the refuse collectors came round, the bins would only be a quarter full, with ash from the fire and maybe a few bones. When you went to buy vegetables from the Frasers' tiny shop – a cramped wooden shack – on the Hereford Road just up from our house, you took your own used paper bags or a frail.

Being careful isn't the same as being mean. To the old shopocracy, waste was a sin, even if you could afford it. They weren't environmentalists by any means, but their way of living was less damaging to the environment than the one we have now.

16

Food was important in our house. My father 'liked his food' and my mother was a good cook of traditional dishes of the kind my father liked. These were rotated according to the day of the week from within a limited repertoire that was never added to as far as I can remember. Sunday would be a big roast – lamb, pork or beef, more rarely chicken which was an expensive meat in the 1940s and early 1950s. Monday there would be cold meat; Tuesday rissoles, if we had had beef on Sunday; if not then perhaps liver and onions. On Wednesday it might be stew in winter or a salad of ham and boiled eggs in summer, chopped up with lettuce, spring onions, tomatoes, and Heinz salad dressing in a big bowl; Thursday, perhaps home-made steak-and-kidney pie (though 'home-made' was axiomatic; my father wouldn't have eaten anything else and it wouldn't have occurred to my mother to try 'bought' meals even after supermarkets wiped out the grocers and greengrocers in the 1960s). Friday was always plaice and chips; Saturday perhaps sausages, or egg and bacon, or lamb or pork chops.

The meat had to be tender, by which my father meant it fell apart in your mouth. If the beef was 'tough', that is if you had to chew it a little, his bottom lip would protrude in a pout and he would chew, as if thinking deeply, knife and fork poised in his fists either side of the plate. Then he would deliver his verdict. 'This meat's a bit tough.' 'I know. Wait till I see Arthur on Monday.' Having grown up with the gold standard of tenderness, I don't like 'tough' meat myself, but I think my father's ultra-pickiness had to do with his teeth. In 1917 he contracted pyorrhoea and the dentist extracted all his teeth. So from the age of fifteen he wore a complete set of false ones. That is so unusual today that for a contemporary fifteen-year-old it would be devastating. My father's generation, though, had a different attitude to teeth. By the time I knew them, none of my aunts or uncles had their own teeth and, likely as not, no one in the broader shopocracy either. It was considered 'natural' to lose them. That was simply what happened and so they accepted it as part of life. In an age with no National Health Service, you only went to the dentist if you had toothache. Brushing teeth (I suspect) would have been a casual affair; 'dental hygiene' and the notion that a full head of teeth can be kept for life, are very much post-1950s developments.

My father would extol the virtues of false teeth. No toothache, no dentist's drills and other agonies, and easy to take out and clean. (He cleaned his once a week or so, and kept them overnight in a glass of water on the mantelpiece, or on the bedside table after he and my mother went over to single beds.) The trouble was, his false teeth were old, from the 1930s and perhaps even the 1920s, with 'gums' the colour of tortoiseshell. He could have got replacements, but my father didn't like change and he was 'comfortable' with these. Over the years, though, the cutting edges of the incisors had become blunt and he could only bite through the tenderest of meat with them. Sometimes, when we were older, he would urge us boys to go over to false teeth, but seeing him grumbling when a raspberry seed got lodged under the top plate, I was never convinced.

Vegetables were still seasonal in the years after the war and one of the pleasures of eating was to follow their progression – the short broad bean season, peas, and later tomatoes grown in our greenhouse and plucked from the vine still warm from the sun; Brussel sprouts, cabbages, cauliflowers that lasted well into the winter, and the winter root vegetables, swedes and parsnips. Only potatoes, onions and carrots were readily available all year round. In spring the first new potatoes, either from my father's garden, or Pembrokes bought from the greengrocer, were considered a particular delicacy, boiled and served with butter. Each year my mother would say 'You can't beat Pembrokes', or if they had been raised in our garden 'Nothing tastes like a newly raised potato; you can't beat home-grown.' My father would agree with a nod, the thick lenses of his glasses steaming up as he leaned over his plate.

Puddings followed a rota too, chosen again from a limited repertoire. Apple pie (or whinberry-and-apple pie in season), tinned peaches and my father's ice cream, stewed rhubarb and custard, stewed gooseberries in season with ice cream; steamed treacle pudding with custard; rice pudding (home-made, not Ambrosia out of a tin).

That was the only form in which my father ever ate rice. For his generation it was strictly a dessert food and he never came to terms with the fact that it is one of the world's great staples. When in later years I would cook an Indian meal and have some friends round, if my father was going through the kitchen to make a cup of coffee for himself and my mother, he would screw his eyes up as he passed, look at the rice and say 'That's not cooked, is it?' There was nothing you could do with rice, he was convinced, except cover it with sugar and milk, sprinkle the surface with cinnamon, and bake it in the oven.

So we ate well, though the emphasis was on meat, with vegetables usually over-cooked because my father liked things 'well done' or 'cooked through'. If Brussel sprouts were even slightly al dente, he would hold one up on his fork for inspection. 'These sprouts aren't done, are they?' Each meal was cooked from scratch with fresh ingredients but a line was drawn with certain basics like bread. My mother was a very good pastry and cake cook, yet she never baked a loaf of bread in her life. Bread was always bought, and had been produced in modern steam bakeries. My mother would often say that 'bread nowadays' was nothing like the loaves Uncle Fred used to bake by traditional methods in the 1920s, but she never tried to rectify the poor quality of 'shop bread' by baking herself. And bread had to be white. On Christmas Day, when my father's brother Don and my aunt Ede and cousins Geoff and Alan came to tea, my mother always had to remember to order a small Hovis for Alan. So there would be one plate piled high with my father's speciality, wafer-thin slices of white bread and butter, and a smaller one for Alan with wafer-thin slices of wholemeal Hovis. This was considered very peculiar on Alan's part; unheard of in fact and a 'fad'. Sometimes one of us would try a slice and would make a face at its nutty taste. 'I don't know how you can eat that, Alan. Wouldn't you like a slice of proper bread?' 'No thanks, Ted.' And then we would forget it till next Christmas. Alan was right, though, as I was to find out. When I was hospitalised in the 1970s in Copenhagen, an X-ray of my intestines revealed that I had acute diverticulosis, the large X-ray plate in hazy shades of grey revealing what looked like a jumbled sky of thunder clouds. 'Poor diet when you were a child,' the consultant commented. 'Lack of fibre.'

Food wasn't just a matter of what was put on the table, though; it was also associated in my mind as a child with charity. Each year we had roast chicken for Christmas dinner, a luxury food until my mother converted in the 1960s to bloated outsized turkeys. ('This meat's a bit dry,' my father would sometimes say about a massive piece of turkey breast on his plate; 'You can't beat chicken.') And each year for many years, she would cook an extra chicken, and just before we ate at one o'clock, my father would take this in the car, together with boiled and roast potatoes, sprouts and mashed swede all wrapped in tin foil, with a jug of gravy, to an old widow in Tudor Street. She would be waiting for him. 'Oh thank you Mr Barnie,' she would say; 'Now you haven't forgotten the stuffing, have you!' Each year, in the week leading up to Christmas, she would put her head round the shop door. 'I haven't forgotten, Mrs ——,' my father would say; 'Chicken all right again this year?' And she would smile and nod.

There were other small acts like this, most of which I never knew about because my father never mentioned them. Like the old lady in Oxford Street, another widow, who he supplied with buckets of coal in winter. I only found out because one day – perhaps my father was ill – he asked me to fill a bucket from the coal shed and take it round to her. When I got to the house, however, there was a car parked outside and the front door was open. I knocked and went in to find the old lady with her hands jammed against the door frame while two people from Social Services tried to prise them away. 'Don't take me away. Don't take me away,' she moaned; 'This is my home.' But 'Come on, dear,' they wheedled, unsticking her fingers from the frame; 'It's for your own good.' And she'd pull her scrawny arms out of their grasp and glue herself to the door frame again. Seeing me, one of the social workers said, 'It's for her own good; she can't cope any more.' I looked into the threadbare kitchen with its worn linoleum floor, the bare table in the middle, the old-fashioned gas cooker, the empty grate. Perhaps it was true. But I went away with her cries in my ears, 'Don't take me away. This is my home,' emptied the bucket in the coal shed and told my father what had happened. 'Aye, poor old soul.' And perhaps he was thinking of his own mother who could have ended up like that, had it not been for him and his brothers and sisters.

Our surroundings define who we are, more than we care to think, and being wrenched from them diminishes us as individuals. That must be one of the most destructive aspects of prison, as it is of what used to be called 'old people's homes' but are now called euphemistically, in the modern way, 'residential homes', *residential* being cunningly elided with *home* to suggest a home-from-home. 'You'll love it here, when you get used to it,' is the implication, whereas the reality is that such places are a human breaker's yard where personality is ripped from its surroundings, from its everyday solidity, waiting for the shell of the body to die.

The generation before my parents', the one born between the 1860s and 1880s, lived in the shadow of the workhouse and feared it. My great aunt May Wood paid sixpence a week until the end of her life into a private insurance scheme, for fear of destitution, even though, when I knew her, the workhouse in Abergavenny was derelict. Both she and Fred were lucky; they had a daughter to look after them in their last, brief illness and they died at Norman Place. My parents too escaped the open prison of the 'home', the rows on rows of the geriatric, slumped with slack mouths before a quietly flickering television set, sleeping away their last days. My father died on a camp bed in the dining room; my mother in hospital.

17

Gardening loomed large for my father as it did for almost every male in his circle. His brother Don had a big vegetable garden on the Mardy, though Fred Wood had the best, a long cottage garden at Norman Place, with apple trees, two rows of black and red currant bushes, gooseberry bushes, and rows on rows of cabbages, sprouts, cauliflowers, carrots, swedes, onions, potatoes and strawberries. Because the Woods were not well off, the garden was an important supplement to Uncle Fred's wages; it must have kept them in vegetables for most of the year.

Each day in summer, after getting home from work, he'd be at the bottom of the garden, bending over the cabbage plants and turning leaves to inspect them for butterfly eggs. Cabbage whites laid their eggs on the undersides in large numbers which he squeezed off with his thumb, moving patiently along the rows. It must have been effective to some extent, but he was always surrounded by a white cloud of butterflies as he bent at his work.

Mr Simpson, the station master, had a more modest vegetable garden at Ross House but during the war and for some years after, he also had an allotment on the Hereford Road, built over now with semi-detacheds. I would meet him in summer, short and corpulent with rolled-up sleeves, wheeling his bike up the Hereford Road, with a spade, fork, rake and hoe balanced across the handlebars, their shafts clutched together over the seat.

Our garden at home, front and back, was given over to flowers. Some of the gardeners must have thought this eccentric. It was all right to cultivate a few flowers. Nearer the house, Fred Wood always had a row of sweet peas, and in front of the coal shed a mass of nasturtiums where I collected black-and-yellow caterpillars that swarmed all over the leaves, keeping them in a jamjar with a perforated greaseproof-paper lid. But flowers weren't considered real gardening; real gardening was vegetables, and whenever we visited Don or Fred or Mr Simpson a little ritual was performed. 'Come and see the garden, Ted.' And all the males would shuffle out of the back door to inspect the neat rows. 'The potatoes look good. And the onions.' 'Aye, but I don't like the look of the cabbages.' 'Club root?' 'Could be.' The women rarely joined in these inspections. Gardening was for the men.

The gardeners of my father's generation would have scorned the fashions of today; the TV makeovers, the decking, the calculated deshabillé of shrubbery and exotics. The old gardeners thought in straight lines, circles, and rectangles, as if part of their job was to bring nature to heel. Straight lines for vegetables, and if you had to have a flower garden, then rectangular beds along the sides of the lawn and a circular one in the middle. That was how our garden was laid out front and back. I wonder if this was an echo of the formal gardens of the seventeenth-century nobility; a descending cultural model which survived among the rural poor and later among the working class and petite bourgeoisie of the towns and suburbs; Romantic informality passing everyone by until the advent of the television-personality gardener.

My father had a strict rotation of plants. In spring multi-coloured tulips, a blousy flower in my opinion, bounced about by the wind; later, sweet alyssum, forget-me-nots, snapdragons, African marigolds, pansies and peonies, and geraniums kept in the greenhouse in pots and planted out each summer. In the larger bed at the back, clumps of perennial daisies with golden petals sprang up each summer. Butterflies and bees and flies loved these, and the garden would be alive with insects. As a child, I would kneel down among the daisies, watching hover flies closely, and red admirals, painted ladies, peacocks, alighting and ticking their wings open and shut as their probosces unscrolled, dipping daintily in the flower heads. Honey bees and wild bees too, and in late summer, wasps, beautiful raiders that hovered round your bread and jam.

This was known as a show. 'You've got a good show this year, Ted.' 'Aye, not bad.' Some went further and competed in the annual flower show in the Drill Hall, or in the horse show held in Bailey Park in the 1950s but later moved to Llanwenarth as it expanded. My father never did this, nor, for some reason, did any of the other gardeners in his circle. When I was a conductor on the Western Welsh, though, I worked with a driver, Jack Case, who did. Mr Case had snowy-white hair and was very quietly spoken. Talking as we climbed from Abergavenny to Brecon in the big maroon bus, I discovered that he was a chrysanthemum fancier. He had a large redbrick house on the side of the Llanwenarth Breast overlooking Llanwenarth and the Usk. We'd pass it on the Brecon bus and he would point it out. There in his greenhouse, Jack Case worked all year on his show chrysanthemums. He was a gentle, patient man, who spent hours after working his shift, tending pots, mixing secret composts, pinching out buds; waiting through the winter months until it was summer again and time to show. 'I'm exhibiting in the Drill Hall on Saturday; why don't you come along,' he asked me once. I was nineteen at the time and gardening was what the men of my father's generation did, standing round in their suits; but I liked Mr Case, so late on that Saturday I went up to the Drill Hall. The judging was over and many of the competitors were packing up. But there was Jack Case, still with his vases of cut exhibition flowers on the wooden trestle. Despite myself, I was impressed. I had never seen such large and brilliant double chrysanthemums. There was a vase of white blooms; another with thick bronze petals curling and tumbling over each other; and another with flowers of the deepest maroon. The petals were still, deep; cool to the touch of the backs of your fingers; more like works of art than flowers. I'd no idea that Mr Case, who I worked with quite often, was rearing such things in his look-out on the hill. 'How did you do?' He smiled and showed me the rosette; First Prize.

My father did grow vegetables but it was in other people's gardens. When Fred Wood became too old to handle his big cottage garden, my father took it over; later when Fred and May had died, he worked the garden of an old lady in Park Crescent. 'Go up and see your father's garden,' my mother said to me once when I was home from Denmark. And I did, and walked around praising the onions and kidney beans. He was pleased. My father and I talked little together and never about anything personal or emotional; our contact was more indirect, standing round a snooker table at the club or looking down on a flourishing row of peas.

Gardening for him was more than a hobby and a source of good vegetables; it was also a dream that would never be fulfilled. Even as a child in the 1950s, I remember him sitting by the fire talking about what he would 'really like to do', and that was to give up the shop and have a market garden. He was a good shopkeeper and kept at it for over forty years, but what he was inside was a gardener and he was happiest on early closing Thursday afternoons when he put on his shabby gardening suit and trilby and went to dig out the tulip and crocus bulbs, replacing them with annuals for the summer 'show'; bringing out the geraniums, two pots at a time from the greenhouse, trilby at an angle. I was working at the kitchen table one day when he walked past, flower pots in hand, and gave me a smile.

The problem was, my mother was a town girl; she liked the shop; and because she couldn't drive, she knew that if they moved out into the country she would be trapped. It never occurred to either of them that she could learn to drive. In the 1940s and 1950s no woman drove among the shopocracy; when Mrs Shackleton learned sometime during the 1960s it was an innovation. The closest my father got to his dream was when one of the redbrick houses on the Llanwenarth Breast, where Mr Case lived, came on the market. High on the hill, it was only a mile and a half out of town and the house had plenty of land. My father even went so far as putting in a bid, but it was too low and while he and my mother debated, someone else bought it over his head. Perhaps it was as well; my mother wouldn't have liked being shut up there, away from the bustle and gossip of the town, even if the house had one of the best views in Wales. She was always more gregarious than my father, always more talkative. He was much more content with his own company.

So he got by with the flower garden at home and the vegetable garden spread at various times across the town. As he grew older, though, the shop became more burdensome, and in summer he started taking the whole of Thursday off to garden; perhaps it was a deal he had struck with my mother who liked being in the shop. When he insisted on retiring at the age of sixty-seven, she wanted to carry on.

Perhaps even he missed the human contact of the shop then, however, because after they retired my father and mother had a much more active social life. Once a week they would play whist with Wilf Trotman and his wife who were 'old friends', though I didn't remember them being mentioned before. In fact, all through my childhood, the only people who called at the house socially, apart from Mrs Shackleton, were family. Others who tried to negotiate an entrance were discouraged. A younger snooker acquaintance at the Con Club had the good idea of parking his wife with my mother a couple of times a week, while he and my father went for a game, but neither my father nor my sociable mother were keen on this. For some time, on Wednesday and Saturday nights, the back garden door leading onto Priory Road would be locked, and we would sit watching television in the dark until we heard the rattle of the knob on the outside door, or the tinny distant ringing of the front door bell in the kitchen. Then we all held our breath. At last, 'I think they're gone,' my father or mother would say, and the central light in the dining room ceiling would be turned on, blinding us.

The lights in the house were all 100-watt bulbs hanging from the ceiling – a standard lamp in the little-used front room was a late acquisition – so if you wanted to read you had to angle your book toward the glare ten feet above you. This didn't bother my parents whose only reading at night was *The Radio Times*. It would be interesting to know how British culture evolved such a friendless form of lighting, the bleak exposed bulb under the shade, shining mercilessly into every face and corner of the room.

Gardening, you would think, would be aligned to an interest in nature, but for the gardeners of the old shopocracy this was rarely so, or in my father's case only ambiguously so. When we drove up the side of the Blorenge on a Sunday afternoon or to the Elan valley to picnic, neither my father nor my mother would stray more than ten feet from the car. On the Whinberry Hill on the Deri they went a little further, but only because there was a purpose, picking whinberries. Till the day he died, he showed no curiosity about the wildlife in his garden and couldn't distinguish a red admiral from a small tortoiseshell, the commonest butterflies that fluttered about his golden daisies; or a blue tit from a great tit as they swirled on the clump of fat and bacon rind he or my mother had hung from the clothesline. Yet in the 1960s and 1970s, his favourite viewing on TV was the never-ending series of BBC wildlife programmes with which David Attenborough established his name. There my father would be, in his easy chair facing the screen, absorbed in the social structure of a colony of baboons, or the life cycle of the great white shark. Over the years, he came into ersatz contact with a huge array of the Earth's varied life, from the teeming species of the Amazon rainforest to the specialised inhabitants of the Namibian desert, yet looking out of the window he couldn't tell you what the bird was pecking crumbs on the sill. 'A sparrow, is it?' he'd hazard, if asked.

If his focus was narrow in the world about him, though, there was something profound in his love of gardening. Handling plants, watching them grow and harvesting their fruits, made him alive to himself in a way that was more difficult to achieve in his dealings with fellow humans. In his final year, as his strength was ebbing, he had to give up the vegetable garden, but he made a heroic gesture, planting broad beans in the flower border opposite our kitchen window, so he could watch them grow. As he lay dying, the large plants with their bluish leaves and cream-and-black flowers thrashed about in the April wind. Associated in folklore and by Sylvia Plath with abundance and fertility, they gave up their pale green beans from the soft fur of the pods after he was dead.

18

Mine was the last generation to be brought up on the concept of Empire. I absorbed this mostly through my mother, though backed up tacitly by my father. For their generation, born at the beginning of the twentieth century, the British Empire was something to be immensely proud of. The sun never set on the Empire I was constantly told, and looking at a Mercator's projection of the world in 1948 with its blocks of deep pink for British 'possessions' spread across the continents, I could see that it was true. The Empire was also unquestionably a 'good thing'. Brought up as Edwardian Empire loyalists, my parents knew that Africans and Indians depended on the benevolent government of the British to provide them with education and health care, but also just to govern them because they were 'incapable' of governing themselves. At the heart of the Empire was the King, and after 1953 the Queen. Queen Elizabeth was our 'best ambassador', venerated wherever she went, especially within the Empire, or the Commonwealth as its shored-up fragments were coming to be known. And watching a Pathé or Gaumont newsreel in the Pavilion or Coliseum as a young teenager, it seemed to be true. Wherever she went on a royal visit, there were crowds of smiling happy faces, warriors with leopard skins leaping in dances of welcome, flourishing assegais and shields while the Queen and a uniformed, plumed, Prince Philip sat in a grandstand covered against the sun and watched. Always a little black girl would run forward and present her with a bouquet of flowers, curtsy and then run back into the crowd.

It was confirmed too through postage stamps. At first I collected indiscriminately, but I eventually specialised in 'British

Commonwealth' which must have been a popular field in the 1950s because Stanley Gibbons issued an authoritative hardback catalogue which I bought every year. Leafing through the thick cream pages of my album, each with its rustling translucent cover sheet, the Queen's head on its elegant swan's neck appeared again and again from Gibraltar to British Guyana, from Australia to Canada, the Falkland Islands and South Georgia, the Solomon Islands, Fiji, Trinidad and Tobago, Jamaica, Barbados, Southern Rhodesia, Northern Rhodesia, Kenya, the Gold Coast, Nigeria, Malaya, Borneo, Hong Kong. All nature's children under the benevolent protection of the Queen.

There was a romance about the Empire which I was not immune to as a child. I spent hours gazing at the stamps in my collection. There were Solomon Islanders putting out to sea in outrigger canoes, red-uniformed Royal Canadian Mounted Police, traditional houses in a clearing in the Brunei jungle, a sheep station in the endless vistas of the Australian outback, all reproduced in the finest colour engravings by de la Rue, London. To a ten- or eleven-year-old, it was an exotic world far removed from the slopes of the Black Mountains and the Usk valley which were home and not exotic at all.

It was not possible to maintain this illusion, though. Weekly the cinema newsreels brought black-and-white footage to our craning faces of atrocities by the Mau-Mau in Kenya, protests in the Gold Coast, soon to become Ghana, the ruthless guerilla war against the Communists in Malaya. Now, when the Queen went on her rounds abroad as our 'best ambassador' and was greeted by warriors in leopard skins, it was to give them their independence, and the dances were to welcome freedom from colonial rule, rather than the adored White Queen of my mother's imagination.

At school for O-level History we studied the History of the British Empire. Looking back it was an anodyne course that glossed over much of the truth. We learned about Warren Hastings' and Clive's intrigues in India, and about the Indian

Mutiny, though not so much about the latter's savage aftermath, and nothing about the disintegration of the Empire that was going on around us. What we studied was the foundation of the Empire and its glory days to the Boer War.

It was impossible not be aware to some extent of what was going on, though, even if it was difficult to interpret. A distant uncle of mine, Bert Wilcock, had fought in the Boer War where he had been wounded in the foot. A portly old gentleman when I knew him, he hobbled slightly and had to have a specially built shoe. He never talked about his war experiences to me, but I was secretly impressed that he had fought against the Boers who I knew from my mother were brave but misguided in their revolt against the British. But then I discovered Deneys Reitz's *Commando* in a blue-covered Penguin. Reitz had fought through the war in a Boer cavalry unit and was one of those who refused to accept defeat and rule under the British, preferring instead exile in Madagascar. *Commando* to a fourteen-year-old was an exciting adventure story, but it was also a revelation, because here was a man who had fought against Uncle Bert, who I thought of as something of a hero. Here was a man who hated the British so much that his family had trekked deeper into southern Africa to avoid us, and who, when overtaken again, fought a bitter war to the end before moving on, because freedom was more important than life.

Recently I reread *Commando*, but the eyes with which I read were different. At fourteen, I had lapped up the excitement of the campaigns, the skirmishes with British units, the narrow escapes. Reitz's attitude to black people passed me by. His was a war of whites against whites, with faithful black 'boys', and African villages of uncertain loyalty that had to be punished, as part of the background. Reitz was probably a benign man by the standards of his day, but *Commando* reveals a thorough racist by the standards of our own and I found it hard to read.

Nonetheless *Commando* was a revelation. If the Boers hated us, with good reason in Reitz's eyes, what about the Mau-Mau and the Malayan Communists? In cinema newsreels they were presented as brutal terrorists, not just the enemies of the Empire but enemies of their own people who 'our boys', the luckless national servicemen of the 1950s, with their white legs protruding from khaki shorts, were out there to protect. I accepted this at thirteen or fourteen. I had no concept that a newsreel could not be telling the truth because I didn't know what propaganda was. For people of my parents' background, the Press, meaning the Conservative Press, always told the truth, and Pathé and Gaumont News were deeply Conservative. So the horrors of the Mau-Mau were reported but not the brutal, large-scale public hangings of suspects by the British. In Malaya, the same national servicemen 'protecting' Malays from Chinese communist guerillas were shown setting jungle ambushes, but not holding up the severed heads of the men they had killed – a photograph of which one of my cousins obtained from someone who had served there.

Then there was the RAF pilot in Cyprus who, rather than bomb Egypt during the Suez 'crisis', drew up the undercarriage of his Canberra bomber on the runway and wrecked it. That impressed me deeply. Nobody would do that, it seemed to me, unless he had an extraordinarily good reason. I began to formulate the idea of individual conscience which might necessitate acting against the tide of public opinion, even against the perceived interests of your country. I don't remember discussing the Canberra pilot with my parents, but if I had, I'm sure they would have seen him as a traitor. 'Why did he join the RAF if he didn't want to serve his country,' my mother might have said. Nasser, to my parents, was a bogeyman like Kenyatta. The Suez Canal was 'ours' not Egypt's; it was vital to our trade routes because Britain was a 'maritime nation' that handled the world's trade in its ships. They weren't aware, or didn't want to see, that the Merchant Navy was effectively destroyed by the Second World War, that the sun, far from never setting over the Empire, was setting over Britain itself, or at least setting over their version of it.

Soon the Empire joined religion as a flashpoint between me and my parents. My mother especially was armoured by imperial propaganda. It took the shape of stories, of caricatures, of assumptions that had never been tested because all her life she had lived in a small-town world where they were accepted as axiomatic. Neither of my parents had any knowledge of the history of the Empire which was seen through a haze of plumed helmets, the thin red line, proud Sikhs and plucky Gurkas, moustachioed colonial officers, pious missionaries. It was all for the best because the Empire was British, and British was best. I was brought up on this too, but by the time I was in Sixth Form, I no longer believed it and pushed angrily at the boundaries of their world view. I can see now that this was unfair. I was beginning to learn the rudiments, at least, of logic, and how books can open the mind to broader perspectives than I had grown up with in a small market town. But I was still too young. At school a group of us debated, or perhaps it would be more accurate to say argued, about politics endlessly; but we were all at the same stage in our development, the contest was equal. With my parents it was different. They had never learned to think abstractly in the way I was struggling towards, so when I raised arguments as to why the Empire was a bad thing, my mother would counter with stories about Baden-Powell who had fought in the Boer War and founded the Boy Scouts and you couldn't say that the Boy Scouts were a bad thing. (As a matter of fact, I could. I had been in the Air Scouts that met each Wednesday in the old church school in Llanwenarth. I had come to dislike their petty rules and chains of command, and when I went to be examined at the Assistant Scout Master's house for my air spotter's badge, I wore long trousers with the rest of my uniform. When I cycled to Llanwenarth the following Wednesday I was told by the Scout Master that I had passed the test but because I had contravened the rules by wearing long trousers, the badge would be witheld for six months. So I left.)

There never was a real discussion with my parents, because we spoke different languages. What started as a challenge on my part became more and more heated until it ended in a row, usually between my mother and me with my father keeping in the background. I should have backed off, but I returned to the attack, angry and inarticulate. Looking back, what did it matter what they believed. But at seventeen or eighteen I was like a terrier with a rag doll and couldn't stop until I had shaken out all the stuffing of what seemed to me the shopocracy's musty beliefs.

19

In Sixth Form I encountered Socialism for the first time among some of the boys from the big estate under the Deri. They were from articulate working-class families, and could produce coherent reasons why Conservatism was wrong. I thought it was wrong too by this time, but more because of the straitjacket the world of the shopocracy had become for me. My reaction was personal and emotional, whereas theirs, even though it was personal too, was ideas- and class-based. Here too the arguments sometimes became heated, especially on my side, because though I was in the process of rebelling against the shopocracy, I wasn't prepared simply to jump ship to Socialism. I did vote Labour once, in 1964, though only to shock my parents. I resisted what might have seemed a logical shift of allegiance partly because I had internalised core attitudes of the shopocracy which I have never been able to shake off. I was suspicious of what seemed to me the levelling down mentality of Socialism, its insistence that the individual subordinate himself to the greater good of the mass. It was a time when I was reading Dostoyevsky, Kafka and Camus, and a book that influenced me immensely, Colin Wilson's *The Outsider*. Wilson spoke, or so it seemed at the time, directly to my experience and my predicament. Struggling out of the confines of the shopocracy's world view, I wasn't about to be trammelled by Socialism and its narrow, programmatic thinking.

So I became, self-consciously, a Wilsonian outsider, in perpetual rebellion against Christianity, the Queen and Empire, Conservatism and Socialism, anything in my small-town world that wanted me to conform. It became a reflex response to new experience – react, don't join; stand on the margins or walk away.

Coming upon *The Outsider* at such a receptive time confirmed me in what were to be lifelong habits of mind, but it could only have done so, of course, if the right material had been there in the first place. The males on my father's side of the family always tended to be loners. My father was invited several times to become a member of the Rotary Club, but he always declined. He wasn't a 'joiner'. When in 1981, the year he died, my cousins and I made the journey to Upper Lybster in Caithness, where our grandfather had come from, we tracked down a cousin twice or thrice removed; one of the last Barnies in the village. He was out in his garden when we called, but seeing strangers approach, he shuffled inside and shut the door. When, instead of going away, as he no doubt hoped, we rang the bell, he opened up and was cautiously and reluctantly friendly. I recognised the pattern.

Sometimes when talking to people, T.S. Eliot's Sweeney comes to mind – 'I gotta use words when I talk to you', or the old blues line 'You can read my letter, but you sure can't read my mind'. Keeping a low profile, not letting the next man know your business, resisting the pressure of the group, were ingrained in the males of our family, even as, paradoxically, they conformed outwardly to the norms of the petite bourgeoisie. In Sixth Form I was in the process of abandoning the one trait and affirming the other. I have most sympathy with Anarchism, though I have no illusions that it could be made to work. In a democracy, if you vote a party into power, you have immediately to join the opposition.

Roundsman, Cynthia Wood, and her father Fred Wood at horse's head, c. 1928.

Left to right: Don, Edgar and Bernard Howse, c. 1941-2. Don was killed in Italy, Bernard badly wounded at Arnhem.

May and Fred Wood at the bottom of the garden at Norman Place, c. 1948.

Christmas night supper. Left to right: Michael Barnie, a girlfriend, Alan Barnie, Geoff Barnie, Ede Barnie, Melva Barnie. Ted Barnie just visible far left, c. 1968.

Tucking in. Ted Barnie at dinner in the kitchen, c. early 1970s. The family were into Pyrex.

Ted and Melva Barnie relaxing in the back garden, c. 1978.

A good show.
My father's flowers in the front (top left) and back garden at Elmsgrove, Hereford Road. Mid 1960s.

Norman Place and its honeysuckle vine.

Left to right: Tim Marsh, Malcolm Eliot, Terence James, John Barnie. *Seated:* Alan Teear. In the grounds of King Henry VIII Grammar School, 1959. St Michael's Convent School in the background.

A pause in the gardening. Mr and Mrs Simpson in the back garden at Ross House.

Thistle Jameson, c. 1900

Andre Gallo, 1930.

20

To the Abergavenny shopocracy, there was no question of being anything other than loyal to the Empire, just as there was no question of being anything other than British. 'We're not Welsh, we're British,' my father would say; or later when I began to question this, 'You're not Welsh, you're British.' Welsh was 'over there', over the looming slopes of the Blorenge and the receding limestone scarp of Llangattock Mountain in the radical mining and steel-making towns and villages. At night, you could see the orange glow of the blast furnaces at Ebbw Vale flaming off the underside of the clouds; there was a constant flow of flatbed lorries carrying steel up the Hereford Road past our house to England.

There was another Wales so remote from us that we had almost no contact with it. Twiddling the knobs of the radio on a Sunday, I would come across a chapel service in Welsh and listen for a moment to the nasal tones of a North Wales preacher, or the sombre waves of a Nonconformist hymn. It seemed so far away I might have tuned in to a station in the Urals or the Caucasus. And there was John Owen y Fenni, an old man then, who wrote poetry in Welsh. He lay dying in the Victoria Cottage Hospital opposite Bailey Park when I visited a friend who was in there for a minor operation. 'Oh yes,' my mother said in the voice she reserved for Literature, 'he's a Bard; he's very well known.'

There were also the place names, Llanddewi Rhydderch, Llanvaply, Llantilio Croesenny, Glangrwyney, Capel-y-ffin, that dwindled away on the road to Monmouth after you passed Raglan, or up the road to Hereford beyond Pontrilas, but thickened and clustered if you went beyond Crickhowell to Brecon, or down to Pontypool or over to Brynmawr. They were more or less mispronounced in the town. Capel-y-ffin was always Capel-y-fin (as in fish fin); and Brynmawr to my mother would never be anything other than Brynmoor. As a child I assumed in fact that *mawr* must be Welsh for *moor* because I didn't believe she could get such a thing wrong. Even when I knew differently and told her what Brynmawr meant and how it was pronounced, it remained Brynmoor. The pronunciation had gone too deep for her to change.

If you climbed the Sugar Loaf, you got another perspective on names. North-west and west were the rolling hills of Wales with their deep valleys; east and north-east the land spread out in blue summer haze with its fields and small woods into Herefordshire and distant Gloucestershire. And there were we in the middle, in the green Usk valley, the town hemmed in by the Blorenge, Llanwenarth Breast, the Rholben, the Deri, Bryn Arrw, Skirrid Fawr and Skirrid Fach (though I only found those last two names much later on an Ordnance Survey map. To the town they were the Big Skirrid or Holy Mountain, and the Little Skirrid).

At my primary school, all the nuns had been English, though they were so purified and otherworldly as a result of their devotion to God, that this seemed neither here nor there. At King Henry VIII's Grammar School, though, the overwhelming majority of the teachers were Welsh, including the headmaster, Mr Newcombe MA (Cantab), an Ebbw Vale man and strict authoritarian. One or two might have been Welsh speakers. Huw Davies, Art, loved to talk of his home patch in Pembrokeshire; Fanny Jones, Biology's, real name was Myfanwy; O-Level History had a Welsh History paper; Wyn Binding, English, introduced us to Dylan Thomas and R.S. Thomas in Sixth Form.

But 'We're British, not Welsh,' my parents would say, and my mother would sometimes add that she had nothing against the Welsh, they were wonderful singers. Hearing a male voice choir on *Songs of Praise* she would say 'The Welsh have the best voices in the world,' or 'You can't beat a male voice choir' with a certain ambiguous air of propriety.

This was something else I began to question in Sixth Form. Though I was deep into D.H. Lawrence, E.M. Forster and Wilfred Owen at the time, Dylan Thomas and R.S. Thomas had a special place in my reading; they spoke to me in a different way, closer, somehow, to where and what I was. When as an undergraduate at Birmingham University, I saw the slim magenta spine of R.S. Thomas's *Poetry for Supper* in the poetry section of the campus bookshop, I felt a thrill of recognition, something that was mine in this English world. I took it down and bought it immediately.

Talking about this many years later with John Osmond who was four years below me at King Henry's (I was in the same class as his older brother Alan), he made the remark that in Abergavenny you can jump either way, making a conscious decision to become English or Welsh. Whichever choice you make, you'll always remain an outsider, a borderer, but in essence John was right. I think you only understand this, though, if you come from the border yourself. When I interviewed Raymond Williams at his home in the Black Mountains for *Planet* just before he died, there was an immediate rapport based on Abergavenny, the Grammar School where he had been a generation before me, and the Black Mountains. He had gone to Cambridge and invented himself as an English academic and I doubt whether for most of his career his Marxist and Socialist contemporaries thought of him as anything other than English; but as his novels show, he had never left the border country in his imagination and in later years he reinvented himself as a Welshman and a card-carrying member of Plaid.

When I left school, my career took me to an English university, then abroad, teaching for thirteen years in Copenhagen where, living in a small self-confident country, questions of identity took on a different aspect. Abergavenny and the borders, though, were always on my mind. For some time I had a tuft of sheep's wool picked up in the Black Mountains, which I would hold to my nose now and then for its muttony smell and which, along with the aroma of a frond of bracken crushed in the hand, is the smell of the border hills to me.

For my parents such sentiments had no meaning. 'Of course you're not Welsh,' my mother would say. And although I knew that deep down there was a sense in which she was right, it would make me angry. My father's father had been a Caithness Scot; what had three generations of hanging around the border made me? My mother's side of the family were Forest of Dean people and therefore, rightly, in their minds, English. Only years later, when I was trying to compile a family tree, did my mother let drop that the Chartist leader, Zephaniah Williams, was a relative. It wasn't talked about by the Forest of Dean Fletchers, my mother's family, because even after all the years, he was considered a blot on the family name. In his pub in Nant-y-glo, Zephaniah had a print on the wall of Christ entering Jerusalem, under which he had written 'This is the man who stole the ass.' Here was one relative, at least, with whom I had something in common.

21

Like most of the shopkeepers, my father was undemonstrative and didn't like 'a fuss'. This must often have frustrated their wives. Whether my father had girlfriends before my mother is unknown, though there was vague talk among my cousins once of a nurse at Pen-y-fal Asylum. He met my mother, in about 1935, in the sweet shop. He used to stay open later than usual on Saturdays to catch people on their way to the first showing at the Coliseum, just round the corner. My mother came in with a group of female friends and he asked her, out of the blue, what she was doing next Saturday night. He probably wanted it to sound casual and spontaneous but, knowing him later in life, he'd probably been plotting it and rehearsing it for weeks, and then just blurted it out.

'That Ted Barnie's a cheeky one,' my mother had said afterwards to her friends, but nevertheless she'd replied that she wasn't doing anything particular, and they started going out.

It was probably a relief to my father to get the courting over; all that disruption to his routine. They married on 22 May 1939, not a propitious time. That would not have been the reason my father insisted on what could only be called a low-key wedding, though. It took place at eight o'clock in the morning at St Mary's, with nobody there except two witnesses, his brother Don and my mother's father, John Fletcher, who must have come over from Lydbrook in the Forest of Dean. It is not known why her mother didn't come as well, though my own mother hadn't lived with her parents since the age of about five. There may not even have been a honeymoon; at least I don't recall my mother ever mentioning one. She talked about the wedding, though, in an amused, slightly chiding way if my father was present. So no bells for my mother, no white wedding dress, no confetti and admiring relations and friends, no wedding feast, and no photographs. Just the 'I do's' before Canon Davies and then off into their life together, the shopkeeper and his new wife.

It was the same with any potential cause for celebration. We boys had proper children's birthday parties until we got too old, but between themselves, my parents just exchanged cards and my mother would get money to buy a dress – 'Well it's what she wants,' he'd say. They may have celebrated their silver and golden wedding anniversaries in some way, but I don't remember either as being anything special and there certainly wasn't a party.

In the same way, they never gave dinner parties. They were not unusual in this; dinner was at 1pm, it wasn't an evening occasion, and this would have been true for all the shopocracy. The notion of inviting friends in for a meal and a bottle of wine simply didn't exist for the petite bourgeoisie of that generation. In the first place, no one drank wine; I don't know where you would have bought it in Abergavenny in the 1940s and 1950s – the chemist's perhaps. Not only that, no one drank any kind of alcohol with a meal. When Mr Trotman and his wife came round to play whist after my parents had retired, they would always have a break for coffee, which meant Nescafé. No one among the shopocracy drank real coffee, and again I don't know where you would have bought it. One of the grocers might have had a small stock I suppose, purchased by the gentry or the prosperous middle class. It was the same with cooking oil. Oil meant fat, half pound slabs of lard that was used to cook everything from fried eggs to chips, from chops to fish. Olive oil was considered medicinal. It could only be bought in tiny bottles at the chemist's. You rubbed it into your ears with cotton wool to loosen hardened wax.

My parents did eat out occasionally, but always when they were away from home; on the one or two occasions when they came to Birmingham when I was a student, for example. If it was at all possible my father made sure that we took our own food. On days out at Barry Island or Porthcawl we always did this. It would have been inconceivable to my father to have eaten out in Abergavenny. Restaurant food was never as good as home-cooked food in his opinion; and since my mother was a very good cook of the kind of food he liked, he had a point. And it is a question where you would have eaten out in the town. In the 1950s there were two cafés, one of which was open at night serving coffee to teenagers like myself and there were two fish-and-chip shops, one of which had a seated area with cheap formica-covered tables, but there was no Chinese or Indian restaurant, in fact no restaurant proper at all apart from in the Swan and Angel Hotels which were open to non-residents. And why would you want to eat in a hotel when you were living at home, my father would have asked, dismissing the possibility. Some of the shopkeepers might have gone into the bar of the Angel for a quiet drink, but none of them would have dreamed of dining there. It was too posh, a cut above them, somewhere where Richard Burton and Elizabeth Taylor had made a legendary overnight stay, which was talked about for years; I wouldn't be surprised if there was a plaque on the bedroom door. It was where I once saw the news presenter, Trevor McDonald, holding forth loudly and self-consciously to a gaggle of media beauties. My mother would have liked that. 'Guess who I saw in the Angel last night.' But the shopkeepers would have scorned it, dipping their cigarettes in the ash tray, and she never got the chance.

My father was normally a reserved man, but when it came to food he would insist on his rights in public in a way that I found embarrassing. One year we switched from Bournemouth to Torquay for our annual holiday. We stayed at a small hotel run by an ex-Royal Navy officer who considered himself a cut above most of his guests. My father had grumbled about the food from the beginning, but things came to a head at the end of the first week when a soft boiled egg I'd ordered for breakfast turned up hard boiled and almost cold. I only pointed this out to my parents, but it was the last straw for my father who, no doubt thinking more of all the meals *he'd* had that were 'rubbish', called the owner over and complained. The ex-Navy man bent down and looked at the egg. 'There's nothing wrong with that,' he said in a scornful way, triggering perhaps a class memory in my father from the war. He used to tell the tale of how, in the army canteen in London, the duty officer would come round and ask in a perfunctory way, 'Any complaints?' Once, my father, having found a worm in the cabbage, stood to attention and said 'Yes, sir!' and showed him the worm. 'Get it down you, man,' the officer had replied. From then on my father got my mother to send him money from Abergavenny so he could eat in the NAAFI. So when the owner of the hotel told him 'There's nothing wrong with that egg,' in the pukka tones of the officer class, it may have hit a nerve, reminding him of the most hateful period of his life, and of the class barriers the petit-bourgeois shopkeeper had to negotiate every day. Sometimes in the shop you had to stand and smile and take it, but my father didn't see why he should pay for the privilege as well. 'That's it,' he told the owner; 'The food and the service here are awful. We're leaving.' And we left the dining room followed by the owner who insisted loudly that we had to pay for the fortnight we had booked. 'Not bloody likely,' my father replied. There was a stand-up row at Reception as my father phoned around, eventually finding another hotel nearby that had a vacancy. 'I'm going to sue,' the owner shouted from the hotel steps as we got in the car. 'Go ahead,' my father shouted back and slammed the door. I can't help wondering if it was the same hotel that inspired John Cleese to write *Fawlty Towers*. The rest of the holiday was fine, but we never went to Torquay again.

This wasn't the only time this quiet man insisted on his 'rights', though it was the most spectacular. In a restaurant in Birmingham once, after a few chews, he pronged a piece of fried plaice on his fork, looked at it, and said 'This fish is raw.' He called the waiter over and insisted he take it away and cook it properly. It came back ten minutes later and the plate was plonked down on the table in front of him. At Ross, coming back from somewhere, we stopped at a teashop and my parents ordered a selection of cakes. They arrived, on a two-tiered cake stand with doilies. Doilies were the epitome of refinement for the petite bourgeoisie; they were de rigeur in the presentation of my mother's cakes at home, so this boded well. But when we tried the selection, we found that the chocolate eclairs were stale and the rock cakes so rock-like that you couldn't bite into them. My father called the owner over. 'These cakes are stale.' 'I don't think so, sir.' 'Yes they are. Look.' 'We don't serve stale food here, sir.' 'Well, we'll pay for the ones we've touched, but not the rest.' 'The charge is all-inclusive for the stand.' 'Well you can forget it. I'm not paying for inedible cakes.' And my father put on the table what he thought the cakes we'd bitten into were worth and got up. 'Come on, I'm not staying here.' 'If you don't pay the full amount, I'll call the police.' 'Call them.' And we trouped out of the tiny tea shop with its lace curtains, the bell tinkling behind us as my father shut the door. All the way to Monmouth, I expected us to be overtaken by a black police car with its bell ringing. 'You can't beat your mother's cooking,' my father would say.

22

The one exception to this what might be called lack of expansiveness was Christmas. On Christmas Eve my parents wouldn't get back from the shop till about 8.30 in the evening. After selling out of Christmas stock, as my mother had predicted, and ensuring that the last Christmas Club parcels had been collected, my father closed up and took my mother and the assistants Nancy and Doreen across the road to the King David for Christmas drinks. The King David must have been one of the oldest pubs in Abergavenny, situated at a point in Frogmore Street that was so narrow there was only room for single traffic. It was torn down in the early 1960s for road widening.

For quite a few years Lil and Bert Wilcock and their unmarried daughter Marjorie came to stay with us at Christmas, travelling down by train from Tipton near Dudley. Lilian was the sister of May Wood, but there was bad blood between them and during their stay they would only go to Norman Place once for a cursory visit, or not at all. As May had had a big hand in bringing me up and was a very gentle person, I sided with her in a sisterly quarrel that went back so far neither of them probably could recall the root of it. Aunt Lil was pleasant enough, but she had a face that implied bitterness and seemed resigned to getting by in life. Uncle Bert, the Boer War veteran, was her second husband, which was considered very unusual. When she was a young woman living in Merthyr Tydfil, her first husband had hanged himself, and she must have moved afterwards to the Midlands where she met Bert. Having a husband who hanged himself was most impressive, and I came to wonder whether perhaps this was the cause of her squeezed-lemon features and the quarrel with May, but I never found out.

Our house had four bedrooms but even so we had to shift around to accommodate everybody. I usually slept in my parents' bedroom with my father. He was an early riser but he must have needed a bit of extra sleep on Christmas morning. He never got it because I would be lying awake in the darkness waiting to hear the bells of St Mary's calling the old ladies and the festivals-only Christians to early morning service. For once I welcomed them because it meant it was nearly dawn. My father who was a light sleeper must have heard them too, because he would always say 'Do you want to open your presents now?' and I would turn the harsh overhead light on and examine the contents of my Christmas stocking while he turned over and tried to sleep.

After breakfast my mother began the big production of Christmas dinner; always stuffed chicken or turkey, boiled or mashed potatoes and roast potatoes, Brussel sprouts, carrots, mashed swede, and thick brown gravy. Then Christmas pudding, home-made by my mother, and white sauce laced with Captain Morgan rum. Back in November my mother made about fifteen puddings and I'd help stir the black treacly mix. Then it was measured out into pudding basins, sealed with greaseproof paper and tied up in muslin. The big corrugated tub in the wash-house would be heated up and the puddings immersed in boiling water where they simmered for several hours. It was a lot of work, but like my father's ice cream, it produced the best Christmas puddings in the town, so everyone said. Some would go to May and Fred Wood, one with the Christmas chicken to the old lady in Tudor Street. We ate our way through the rest on Sundays during January and February. Christmas puddings lasted for months. 'You can't beat your mother's Christmas puddings,' my father would say, spoon in hand, pouring the pungent rum sauce over his dark brown, glistening slice.

After it was over, my father, Lil and Marjorie did the washing up – a big production again because the tiny scullery where my mother cooked was piled high with saucepans, lids, roasting trays, plates and serving dishes, knives, forks and spoons. Then, bloated and exhausted, everyone sat back and had a cup of tea and all the adults retired to the dining room to fall asleep, leaving me and my brother playing in the kitchen, or outside if it had been snowing.

Christmas dinner was one climax of the day, but it was only the build-up to something bigger. Round about four in the afternoon, the fire was lit in the front room, the only time in the year that this was done. The room was dominated by the quarter-size snooker table, with the sofa pushed into the bay window and the two armchairs crushed up against the wall either side of the fire place. There was my mother's glass-fronted china cabinet too, with the delicate bone china she had been given as a wedding present. So when we played snooker, it was difficult to make a shot from certain angles, one knee up on the arm of the sofa, or backed up against the china cabinet with the cue angled down at ninety degrees to the cue ball to get any kind of shot at all.

But on Christmas afternoon we weren't getting ready to play snooker. At half-past four the back door would open and in came my father's favourite brother, Don, his wife Ede, and my two older cousins Geoff and Alan. Geoff worked at Pilkington's glass works at Pontypool and later, when that closed, at Pilkington's new glass fibre factory at New Inn. Alan was a printer at Sergeant's. There would be handshaking all round and then we squeezed into our seats at the kitchen table which had been set for Christmas tea with my mother's best china, the only time of the year it was ever used; tiny cups that were so thin you could almost see through them, with little handles you could hardly grip. Petit bourgeois chic of the 1930s.

Because this was teatime, tea was served, the one exception to the no-drinks-at-mealtimes tradition of our family, and my father, whose chair was nearest the scullery, would be up and down boiling kettles, stewing the peat-coloured brew. Christmas tea was always the same. Tinned peaches and cream first, eaten with slices of my father's wafer-thin bread and butter. It was a firm conviction of my father's that if you ate tinned fruit without bread and butter it would give you indigestion. We boys would protest but it wouldn't do. 'No, come on; you can't eat peaches without bread and butter.' Then there would be the cakes, all home-made by my mother. Fairy cakes, some sprinkled with hundreds and thousands or little threads of milk chocolate – what a farmer in the shop one day called 'mouse droppings' when he couldn't think of the name. 'Give us a quarter of those mouse droppings, will you, Mrs Barnie?' It was one of my mother's favourite shop stories, together with the one about the woman boasting of her 'cruise'. 'How was your cruise, Mrs ——?' 'It was wonderful, Mrs Barnie. We had an aperient before dinner every evening.'

There would be a plate of Welsh cakes, too, baked on a big cast-iron bakestone on top of the stove, and my favourite, chocolate eclairs covered in melted milk chocolate and filled with cream. 'Have another eclair, Ede.' 'Oh no thank you, Melva; I've got to leave some room for the cake!' And there it would be in the middle of the table, my mother's Christmas cake, made at the same time as the puddings, the succulent rich cake covered with marzipan and coated with snow-white icing, smoothed across the top with a warm knife while it was still wet. Using an icing syringe, she would pipe a squiggly decoration around the top and in zig-zags on the sides, in pink or blue. The cake tasted lovely but it was always an ordeal, even for us boys. 'Just a small slice for me, Melva, please.' 'Oh I couldn't, Melva, thanks. I'm bloated.' 'Oh go on, Bert, just a little bit. Just to taste.' 'Oh all right then.'

Tea was fine, but it was something to be got through to the exciting part. While the women washed up, the rest of us moved into the unfamiliar warmth of the front room. There a heavy, four-piece, polished wooden top had been placed over the snooker table and the front room was ready to be turned into a gambling den. Flagons of beer and glasses were brought in and shallow champagne glasses in case the ladies wanted a Babycham, and sherry glasses for the sweet brown sherry. Each of us processed down the hall with a kitchen chair. 'Got the cards, Ted?' And a pack would be produced to the rattle of small change as the men emptied their pockets onto the table in front of them. We boys were allowed to play too, and had our stakes of pennies and halfpennies, brass-coloured threepenny bits, silver sixpences, shillings, two shilling pieces, and halfcrowns. Flagons were opened and bitter-smelling glasses of beer passed round, except to Uncle Bert who always had a whisky with a dash of soda. 'That enough soda for you, Bert?' 'Just right, Ted, thank you.' And the men talked in a desultory, waiting kind of way, until the women appeared from the scullery and took their places. The cards were then shuffled and my father dealt them round the table, face-up, until someone got a jack. He or she would be the first banker. It was usually a man, though, the women preferring to sell the bank if the jack landed with them. 'Anybody want to buy it?' And there'd be a brief flurry of bids, the new banker shuffling the cards and announcing the rules. 'Ace high, five-card trick beats a straight pontoon, aces can be split, half a crown limit.' And as Bert lit up a big fat cigar which he was only allowed at Christmas, the cards would be dealt round the table. 'Place your bets!' – this to the women, who apart from my mother, were only half-heartedly interested in the game, Ede turning to Lilian to say something, while pennies and halfpennies were pushed out in front of the cards. 'All done?' The second card would then go round, the dealer leaning forward to each of us in turn as we stuck, bought, twisted or bust.

Cigarettes were lit, and there was soon a smokey haze over the table. When someone got a royal pontoon, he took the bank and there'd be a pause while the new banker shuffled the cards. Another flagon was opened. 'A top-up, Bert?' 'No thanks, Ted. I'm all right, thank you.' The new banker would declare his maximum stake, 'Five shillings,' and we'd start again. When we boys got older, and the evening wore on and the drink flowed, the bank became more reckless. 'Five pound limit.' And if someone had two aces which they split, with five pounds on each, 'This is real gambling!' my father would half-grumble with a pout.

In between hands, there was talk and jokes. 'Aye, she was all tit-and-bum,' my cousin Geoffrey might say, describing a woman he knew, as he leaned forward and pushed his backside out. 'Yer's my 'ead; my arse is coming!' And my father might recite again the limerick he'd learned as a grocer's apprentice during the First World War, which ended:

> But it wasn't the Angel of God,
> It was Roger the Lodger, the sod.

'But they do a lot of good,' my mother might be overheard saying to Ede about the Salvation Army. She was always saying that when I tried to argue religion with her. 'But what about the Salvation Army? You can't deny they do a lot of good.' Geoff, who would be poised to deal their second cards, would join in. 'Rubbish!' and off he'd go on a story about the Sally Army Major you'd see collecting in Red Square, a real Holy Joe; but a telephone engineer he knew had been up a pole one day on the Pontypool road and had seen the Major with an Army woman in the back of a car in a lay-by. 'He was on his knees, but he wasn't praying. – Load of bloody hypocrites,' Geoff, who had an anti-Christian streak, would conclude. 'Anyway, place your bets; let's be having you!' And my mother and Ede would have to look at their cards again, Ede leaning over to show hers to my mother. 'Oh put a penny on it, Ede.'

At ten o'clock it was back to the kitchen where the fire had been kept in and the table re-laid for supper; and the men took the chairs down the hallway again. It was always the best meal of Christmas – slices of cold ham, cold chicken or turkey from dinner, with cold stuffing on the side, a big pork pie and a wedge of cheddar cheese; Branston pickle, pickled onions, pickled beetroot, and the Christmas speciality, pickled walnuts. Plates of bread and butter would be handed round. 'Come on, everybody,' my father would urge, 'help yourselves!'

My parents' generation was the great generation of smokers. All the shopkeepers smoked and so did most of the wives. My father introduced my mother to cigarettes when they were courting, and in the mid-1930s it must have seemed glamorous to her, like the film stars who pouted through a haze of smoke, cigarette held between manicured fingers at shoulder height. She was born in 1908 and very few of the women in our circle born a decade or so earlier ever smoked – Ede, May Wood, May Hodges – though my father's younger sisters, Hetty and Jess, did. I imagine that May Wood and Fred would have disapproved strongly, though Fred of course smoked. But for my father and mother's generation, smoking was sophisticated, part of modernity.

They were comparatively moderate smokers, fifteen or twenty a day perhaps, but the ceilings of the kitchen and dining room, where they smoked most, would be stained brown with nicotine after a couple of years and would have to be repainted.

From as early as I can remember, I hated smoking – from the smell of the phosphorus on the match heads to the acrid cigarette smoke and the ashtrays stuffed with stubbed out ends. It smelled and looked horrible to me and once when I watched one of the adults stub out a cigarette in the yoke of a discarded fried egg, I was almost sick. Worst of all was when my parents smoked in the car where there was no escape from the enclosed stench. If I surreptitiously opened the back passenger window to get some fresh air, I would soon be told to close it because of the draught. So there my parents would be in front, my mother lighting up two cigarettes and passing one to my father, while they both looked ahead at the unwinding road, and me in the back trying to hold my breath, then letting it out in a burst and having to suck in their dirty air despite myself.

Later on, if my mother had Mrs Shackleton around for a coffee evening, perhaps with their old school friend Mrs Garner, the room would be dense with cigarette smoke and the aroma of stale perfume and lipstick. At the Con Club, everyone smoked. 'Have a coffin nail,' they joked. But Don died of stomach cancer and both my parents developed hacking, phlegm-laden coughs in their later years. 'I'm giving this game up,' my father would say, as he hacked into a handkerchief, and eventually both he and my mother did stop. As he lay dying, his lungs constantly filling with fluid, he wished he'd stopped long before. 'Smoking's a mug's game,' he reflected, too late.

In their prime, though, this never entered the heads of the shopkeepers and their wives. So after we got up from the supper table and heaved the heavy kitchen chairs back down the hallway once more, they would all light up in the densely smokey room, except Alan and Aunt Ede who never smoked. 'Who's banker?' And whoever had the bank before supper would deal the cards and we'd carry on.

If my father went out down the hallway to the kitchen for another flagon of beer or a coffee for the women, he would sometimes let out a rip-roaring fart, if he thought he was alone. If you were behind him, 'Ah, that's better,' he might say, or quote a verse

Wherever thou art, let the wind blow free,
For the want of a fart was the death of me

which he said was on a tombstone in the graveyard at Longtown. I cycled out there once to look, but couldn't find it. Perhaps it was on a par with my father's comment when we played snooker. If someone narrowly missed a pot – 'They'd give you that in Cwmyoy,' he'd say, as he leaned on his cue.

We broke up about midnight or half past when someone, usually my father, would shout 'Last bank!' So when the next royal pontoon was turned up, the cards were stacked and we'd count our profit or loss. The bank almost always did best, especially if you had it toward the end of the evening. 'How did you do, Alan?' 'Oh not bad, Melva; about two quid up I reckon.' 'I'm down by about a fiver.' 'Me too,' someone would say. After he was old enough to play, my teenage brother, by careful betting and on occasion extraordinary runs of luck, would amass quite a stack of silver and banknotes. At some point in the evening, counting it up, he'd say, 'Well, I'm off to bed now. Goodnight everyone.' There'd be a rumbling of discontent, because if you'd had a good bank you were supposed to play on so that everyone had the chance of winning it back. This wasn't a casino. But it was soon forgotten. 'Right, eyes down – first cards coming round; place your bets!' and we'd carry on.

When the last game was over, we filed back out to the kitchen and coats and hats were handed round from the hooks under the stairs, then we'd go out to see Don, Ede, and Geoff and Alan off. Sometimes it had snowed while were playing and they'd decide to walk, leaving the car to be picked up next morning. We watched them trudge off through the deserted streets, snow squeaking under their shoes as they made tracks in the whiteness beneath the glitter of the stars.

On Boxing Day we all went up to the Mardy, or after Don died in the mid 1950s, across to Chapel Road where Ede and my cousins moved when the shop was sold, and the ritual of tea, gambling and supper would begin all over again.

23

Health was always a concern of the Barnies, and it would be fair to say that many of them were hypochondriacs. 'Hope for the best, but expect the worst' might have been the motto of my father and his brothers and sisters. At least they didn't have their teeth to worry about, but everything else was fair game. For years in the late 1940s and early 1950s, my father had a persistent pain on one side of the small of the back, which he was convinced was cancer of the kidney. It doesn't seem to have occurred to him or anyone else that cancer of the kidney would have killed him off years before. Instead he went again and again to his GP who put him through every test he could devise without finding evidence of cancer or anything else. Eventually his doctor advised him to make an appointment with an eminent Harley Street specialist, Dr Nanda. I expect that despite his worries, my father would have balked at this on grounds of expense and the necessity of going all the way to London, a place he disliked. My mother, who had taken the brunt of his worrying, insisted however, and so they went on the train to Paddington Station and Harley Street.

Dr Nanda, my father had to admit, gave him a very thorough examination, coming to the conclusion that the pain was a result of one leg being slightly shorter than the other which was putting pressure on the spinal column in the small of the back. The solution was a special insole in the one shoe. 'Well, that's a relief,' my mother said as they walked past the railinged façades of Harley Street. 'Bloody fool doesn't know what he's talking about,' my father replied. At which point (my mother said) she threatened to divorce him. Whether it was the threat of divorce or that, deep down, the specialist's advice rang true, the pain went away and there was no more talk of cancer for a while.

Cancer, though, was always a spectre for the Barnies. My grandfather, John Henderson, almost certainly died of it, as did my father's brother, Don, in 1955 when he was only sixty-one. He'd gone into hospital with severe abdominal pains, but when they operated they found a cancer in the stomach too far advanced to remove. So they stitched my uncle up again and he went home to die. It was a lingering death, Don being unable to keep any food down, so he got thinner and weaker as the days and weeks dragged by. Sitting with some lightly scrambled eggs while the rest of the family ate a roast beef Sunday dinner, 'I'd give anything to be able to eat that,' Geoff recalled him saying.

When he was near death, my parents went up to the Mardy, and I cycled from school to May and Fred Wood's at Norman Place. My mother and father came to pick me and my brother up around nine that evening, everyone crowding into my aunt and uncle's tiny living room. 'Aye, he's gone, poor Don,' was all my father could say. It was one of only two times I saw him cry.

Unsurprisingly, though they all worried about their health, especially the males, they were very hazy about what might be called the geography and functions of the body. My father and mother frequently speculated about the cause of Don's cancer, my father perhaps thinking that if they could work that out he could take prophylactic action himself. Worry was one theory; endless worry about the Mardy shop and post office. Another, and the one my parents tended to favour, was that one day not long before the onset of the disease, Don had been trying to open a tin of ham in the shop. The lid had been jammed on tight and, holding the tin close to his body, a corner of the lid had jabbed him in the stomach when it flew off suddenly. It is what might be called the 'bruise theory' of cancer. It has not caught on, so far as I know. My parents were convinced, however. 'Aye, he was never the same again,' my father would say reflectively. Smokers themselves, it never occurred to my parents that a lifetime's heavy smoking may have been the cause of Don's cancer. The dangers of smoking were becoming known in the 1950s but they weren't yet widely publicised, and the shopkeepers of Abergavenny smoked on in happy ignorance.

Nervousness, or 'nerves', was a family trait, especially among the Barnie males and it would have been no surprise to them that the cancer went to Don's stomach. The stomach was their weak point. The shopkeepers weren't letter writers – I only had a letter once from my father after I left home, on a torn-out sheet of an old invoice book, 'E.C. Barnie, Wholesale and Retail Confectioner' – but my father kept a letter he received from his brother Bill. The letter is undated, but was written just before Christmas, 1949.

<u>Sunday</u>   Ward 5
                                                 Royal Gwent Hospital
                                                 Newport
                                                 <u>Mon</u>

Dear Ted and Melva,

I hope you are all well: you may be surprised to see above address on this letter. I have been here a week; and am having an operation for the ulcer, Tuesday 9.00. The last ulcer has apparently left a deep crater, and another one might penetrate the stomach wall, with very serious results. So I hope my trouble will soon be over for good. This will be my first Xmas spent in a hospital. I hope I will get a little bit of Xmas dinner. I have had a Blood transfusion, stomach tests and all kinds of curious tests this last week. They are pretty thorough here in every thing. I hope you will all have a very happy Xmas. Love to John, Michael, and yourselves – from

<u>Bill</u>

This was probably his last communication with my father.

Extrapolating from the rest of the family, it's not hard to imagine Bill's feelings of disorientation and isolation in the Royal

Gwent. All the Barnie males were small-town individualists who guarded their independence. The obverse of keep your business to yourself was don't meddle in other people's and keep clear of authority. The Army was authority and my father had hated it. Doctors and hospitals were authority too; an alien world with its own mysteries, where if you got into their power you were not only made to feel socially inferior, you were made to feel that you were nothing at all; something to be worked on, operated on, your personality and your inner needs disregarded.

Many years later, in the 1970s, I went with my father to Nevill Hall Hospital in Abergavenny where he was to have a series of tests. I waited in the desolate corridor while he went into a room to change, emerging in his old-fashioned brown dressing gown which he never wore at home. His glasses flashed as he threw a nervous smile in my direction, all his confidence gone. It was decided that an operation was necessary. I never found out for what, but I suspect it may have been some form of cancer. In hospital recuperating he was a very bad patient. If restaurant food was bad, hospital food was worse. 'The food here is bloody awful,' he'd complain when you visited, his bottom lip protruding in a characteristic pout. It was no use telling him he wasn't there for the food. After the operation, he had come round from the anaesthetic to find tubes down his throat and sticking out of his arms. Thrashing about, he pulled them all out, twice. 'I'm not having this!' 'It's for your own good, Mr Barnie,' the nurses had said. He was discharged shortly afterwards and recuperated at home, the nurses no doubt glad to be rid of him.

Bill, alone in a large hospital in Newport with Christmas coming on, must have felt something like this. In his letter, he may have been putting a brave face on his situation. After a stomach operation, there would have been no taste of Christmas dinner for him; but the operation was not a success, and he died in the Royal Gwent on Christmas Day, aged fifty-one. A cutting from a Monmouth newspaper records the funeral –

The Late Mr. W.G. Barnie
Many friends attend funeral

The funeral of Mr. W.G. Barnie, of 2, Oakfield, Hereford-road, Monmouth, took place at Monmouth Cemetery on Thursday afternoon last. He died on Christmas Day at the Royal Gwent Hospital, Newport, at the age of 51 years after several months illness. He was the son of the late Police-sergeant J.H. Barnie, of Monmouth.

Prior to the interment, a service was held at St. Mary's Church where the Vicar (Canon E.P. Knight) officiated. The hymns sung were 'How bright these glorious spirits shine' and 'Now the labourer's trials are o'er,' also Psalm 23. In paying tribute to Mr. Barnie, Canon Knight referred to his popularity and to his keen sense of devotion to duty.

His keen sense of devotion to duty. The family would have appreciated that, as would the Mayor, Alderman N.C. Elstob, and Councillor and Mrs. G. Manns, the Rev. A.H. Sayers, Major A. Reade D.S.O., M.C., Lieutenant Colonel W.C.N. Lee, Mrs H. Cullen-Jones (representing the women's section of the British Legion) and a crowd of other Monmouth townspeople who packed St Mary's Church that day. Devotion to duty, uprightness, the rigid code of the shopkeepers.

24

Sometimes life can seem to be flowing in a predictable course and then something detonates, like dynamite thrown casually into a pond, and everything changes. In the summer of 1966 I came down to Abergavenny by train from Birmingham, where I was studying for an MA, to spend a couple of weeks at home. I arrived to find my parents deeply worried about my younger brother Michael; he was behaving 'strangely'. They took me into the front room where on top of the upright piano there was a white porcelain bust of Beethoven which belonged to my brother. Only, Beethoven's wild hair and driven, furrowed face had been crudely sprayed with gold paint. My parents said he was talking all the time and doing odd things and they couldn't get any sense out of him. Could I have a word.

My brother was four-and-a-half years younger than me, born in 1945 at the end of the war. My father was still away in the Army when in the early hours of the 29th of August my mother felt herself going into labour. There was no phone in the house – we didn't get that till the mid 1960s – so leaving me with a young girl who was living in and helping around the house, she walked by herself two hundred yards down the Hereford Road to the Victoria Cottage Hospital. There she gave birth at once to my brother who was severely premature. At birth he weighed only two pounds – like a bag of sugar, my mother used to say. She had walked to the hospital in a violent thunderstorm which had me running to the girl's room at home, where I burrowed under the sheets to the foot of the bed. Alone in the house with a four-year-old, she was probably as scared as me. 'Oh Mrs Barnie, you shouldn't have walked down here alone,' the nurses had said; but there had been little choice.

In 1945 there were no incubators, at least there were none in the Cottage Hospital, so the nurses dressed my brother in dolls' clothes to keep him warm and thanks to their care he lived. It must have been an anxious time for my parents, and for me it was disorienting. I don't remember being told that I was going to have a brother, though I must have been. When, after a week, my mother was due out of hospital, my aunt, May Wood, came round to the house to help prepare for her homecoming. That was very unusual. As a young woman she had developed a carbuncle behind her right ear. It could easily have been removed surgically, but probably from a fear of doctors and hospitals, she had refused to have it done. As a result it grew to the size of a grapefruit, and though in the 1920s she had been a shop assistant at Stoneham's the grocers, for all the years I knew her, she never went beyond the gate of Norman Place. The railings at the front and the brick wall at the bottom of the garden marked the beginning and the end of her world. So my mother's coming home from the Cottage Hospital must have been exceptionally important to her. I remember me and my aunt waiting and then my mother came through the back door and into the dining room where she sat down in the easy chair with its back to the window. I ran to scramble onto her lap, but my aunt held me back; 'Not now, John, your mother hasn't been well.'

It was a long time before my brother was brought to the house, and I may even have forgotten about him. I was certainly oblivious to what must have been a lot of anxious talk between my parents. I can only remember a darkened room and a cot and being told to tiptoe up to see him.

But my brother survived, and though he was 'delicate', as my mother put it, we joined the two-child families which were becoming fashionable in the years after the war. Because of the age difference between us, though, there was an inevitable gap between my brother and myself. I was about to leave primary school when he started in the Infants' class; when he was in First

121

Form at the Grammar School, I was in Fifth Form studying for my O-levels; by the time he went to Newport College of Art, I was about to start my MA in Birmingham. So because we were out of kilter in terms of our development and developing interests as children and teenagers, we tended to move in different spheres.

As far as I was aware, everything had been going well with my brother's art studies at Newport, but at the end of his second year the detonation happened. It was the time when Op Art and Pop Art were the latest trends, and at Newport College of Art, you were either an Op or Pop artist, or you were nothing. My brother did the exercises he was told to do, but there was a side to him, influenced by Huw Davies, the Art master at the Grammar School, which liked more conventional painting too. At the end of the second year, the students exhibited their work in one of the College's studios, their three-dimensional structures set out on trestle tables. One of the lecturers, S——, a leading Op artist of the day, entered the room and walked around examining their work. When he came to my brother's, he took a look at it and then set fire to his structure on the trestle table. Humiliating your students is unforgivable in a teacher, though in the atmosphere of the mid 1960s at Newport it no doubt passed for witty criticism. What he couldn't have known was the devastating effect this would have on my brother.

Michael had been out when I arrived, but when he returned he took me immediately to the front room and started to talk in a way I had never known before. Non-stop talk. Wild talk. Talk where he didn't appear to pause for breath. Talk that leapt from pun to pun like stepping stones over a torrent as he jabbed me excitedly with his finger. I tried to slow him down, to reason with him, but the only reason he was open to was his own – how the Masons were after him; how washing hoisted high on a clothesline across Priory Road was a coded signal; how they had broken in and stolen his things. I tried to tell him that this couldn't be, that the Masons didn't do things like that and in any case why would they be after him. But from where he was standing, what I said was insane; it was obvious; couldn't I see. I realised that the only way to engage with him was to accept that the Freemasons were conducting a clandestine vendetta against him. And there was no end to their ingenuity. If a new *Yellow Pages* was left on the doorstep, it was a message from the Masons – 'YOU'RE YELLOW'. On a later occasion, signing himself in at Maindiff Court Psychiatric Hospital, he wrote 'Paranoia, caused by the Masons' as the reason for his illness. The Masons were never far away when he fell into the abyss

If I was out of my depth, my parents were even more so. A neighbour had knocked on the door and said 'Mr Barnie, you'd better come and see to your boy. He's lying in the gutter in Priory Road.' And there he had been, curled up. He'd thrown himself flat, he said, when the Masons had attempted a drive-by shooting. He had gone up to the store on the corner of Hereford Road and Park Crescent and had ranted non-stop at the owner who had no doubt got scared and told him never to come back. Nothing like this had happened before in my parents' small-town world; they operated within the shopkeepers' perception of 'things as they are', and things went on in a predictable round of days and weeks and months and years. But here, suddenly, the door was kicked down, and they didn't know why, and they didn't know what to do about it. So they hoped when I got home that I would be able to reason with my brother, to 'talk him out of' his strange behaviour. But there was no talking to him because, in the first place, he was the one doing the talking in a fountain display of ingenious associations, word-play, jokes, words tumbling over each other as if one mouth wasn't enough to communicate the speeded up nature of his thoughts. To have talked with him, I would have had to enter his skewed world that operated at its own pace and with its own logic; I would have had to close the door on my own sanity for a while in order for us not to talk past each other. I tried it once, accepting his premises, seeing where it led; but it led nowhere because there was no thread there which could be used to entice him back into our world; instead I could see that it was possible to lose my own footing, as if I was wading deeper and deeper into a fast-flowing river.

Hours passed and it got dark. I had been consulting with my parents in the kitchen when we suddenly realised that we didn't know where my brother was. Had he slipped out? I went upstairs from room to room and found him in one of the first storey bedrooms, lying on the floor with his legs together and his arms spread out, as if he was being crucified. The skin on the palms of his hands was criss-crossed with deep cracks like the bed of a reservoir or lake after a prolonged drought. He lay there clenching his teeth, as if hanging on, saying nothing.

I went back down to the kitchen and told my parents that we had to get him into Maindiff. I don't know why it took me so long to realise this. Perhaps it was because I thought it was a temporary aberration, that if we talked it through with him we could persuade him out of this delusion about the Masons, that he would become one of us once more. But I knew nothing about manic depression or schizophrenia and didn't realise that when I arrived home he had been on a high for several days and that now, lying crucified upstairs, he was plunging into a desperate depression. What I had, at last, learned from the day was that talking and reason could do nothing against the powerful engine that was driving him on.

So my father got his coat and hat and we drove up the dark Ross Road to Maindiff Court. Rudolf Hess had been imprisoned in the old Court there during the war, and there were many tales told locally of seeing him on walks with his guards in the lanes around Tredilion and the Mardy. But after the war, the old mansion had been demolished and Maindiff Court Psychiatric Hospital built in its place, with its brick buildings named after the surrounding hills.

Maindiff was an adjunct to Pen-y-fal Asylum which had been a

124

dominating presence in my childhood. Built in the nineteenth century of local sandstone, Pen-y-fal looked like a prison. Standing in the garden of Mr and Mrs Simpson's house at the end of Priory Road I could look out over the River Gavenny sunk deep in its banks and over the high wall that surrounded the exercise yard. I would stand fascinated by the figures I saw there, listless in drab grey uniforms, or screaming and shouting, their voices echoing across the hiss and roar of the river as it pounded over a waterfall below. Behind them were the high, barred windows of the main building which were lit up at night so that from a distance it seemed like a palace. From the Simpsons' garden, though, you could see the disembodied heads and shoulders of people passing now and then from window to window and could wonder what they were doing. When someone escaped, the asylum siren sent up its mournful wail, and wardens in black uniforms and peaked caps went up and down the streets knocking on doors and warning that there was a patient 'on the loose'. If you lived on our side of the town, you could not ignore Pen-y-fal.

In the 1940s and 1950s there were several hundred people in Pen-y-fal, in the night-time palace of lights shining behind the horse chestnut trees that overshadowed it, where the rooks nested in spring, rising at dusk in huge cacophonous flocks that flew out over our house before returning in the fading light to roost. But by 1965, Pen-y-fal was beginning a long process of being wound down; drugs and ECT were revolutionising psychiatric practice, and Maindiff Court had become the centre of mental health care in the town. So it seemed natural to go there for help.

Steering along the winding roads of the hospital grounds, we found the main building and were eventually shown into the office of the duty psychiatrist. He didn't ask us to sit down, so we stood in front of his desk, my father twisting the rim of his hat in his hands while I told the doctor what had happened. He listened non-committally and when I had finished told me that we had come to the wrong place. We hadn't followed proper procedure;

we should have called our GP and if he thought the case warranted it, he would alert the Mental Health Authority and then perhaps my brother would be admitted to Maindiff. I pointed out that we didn't know this and that my brother was in a desperate situation that seemed to be getting worse and worse, but he stone-walled me. We had to follow proper procedure.

One of the things the old shopkeepers hated above everything else was 'a fuss', a confrontation where the gloves are pulled off and you face another person with open hostility. If you run a shop it is necessary to avoid this; the customer isn't 'always right' by any means, but you have to pretend that he is, and the shopkeepers had many stratagems to back away from or to divert potentially explosive situations. The son of shopkeepers, I have internalised this view of human relations. The trouble is, if you repress your true feelings again and again, something (and it may be something that seems insignificant to others) will act as a trigger that causes you to lash out in a spasm of anger and aggression that takes the recipient completely by surprise. It's what happened to my father in the hotel in Torquay, and it happened to me then in that psychiatrist's office. Normally I would have backed down and said 'Oh I see; I'm sorry, we didn't realise.' But suddenly I hated him, sitting there impassively, impregnable behind his petty 'procedures', while my brother was lying in the bedroom, arms stretched out as if they had been nailed to the floorboards. So I got extremely angry and started arguing back. But it was too much for my father, face to face with authority. He pulled at my sleeve and said 'Come on, let's go,' and we went back out into the night, driving in silence down the long winding gradient of the Ross Road, past where the old LMS Junction had been, past the railway cottages, toward the glittering lights of the town.

When we arrived back at the house we were lucky enough to contact our family doctor; perhaps he had been on night call that week. He drove round straight away and I took him upstairs to the room where my brother had kept his cruciform shape for several hours. The doctor crouched beside him and asked my brother some questions to which he got no answers. 'Yes, we need to get Michael hospitalised straight away,' he said. He reached into his bag and filled a syringe, injecting my brother in the arm with what I took to be some kind of sedative. Between us we managed to get him on his feet and down the stairs to the doctor's car. They drove off down Priory Road. Proper procedure had been observed.

There followed days and weeks of treatment at Maindiff Court. For a long time my brother was on drugs that sedated him; he slept immensely, deeply, yet woke up washed out and exhausted. He was fed glucose and given ECT, which he came to dread. The large amounts of glucose bloated his body, the ECT wiped his brain of all recent events. When we started to talk about what had happened, we found that he could remember nothing. For some days he was in a locked room and it was there, as he sat by the bed where my brother lay in a deep slumber that I saw my father cry for the second time.

The summer was coming to an end and my brother should have been preparing to go back to the art college for his final year, but of course there was no question of that. My parents must have contacted the college to let them know what had happened; I had gone back to Birmingham by then. The principal asked my father to go down to Newport to see him. He would have been daunted by this, taken out of his world again and brought face to face with authority.

He was led into the principal's office where the principal came forward to shake his hand. There was another man present who he introduced as Mr S——, the lecturer who had burnt my brother's work and precipitated his breakdown. He too offered to shake hands, but my father refused. It was his one gesture of protest at what had happened. The principal said that he was sorry to hear of my brother's condition and that of course he would be able to defer his final year until the following autumn.

And that was that. If it happened today and if my parents were middle class, the college would likely as not be sued. But that was not how things were done in the 1960s and my parents would in any case have disapproved of the culture of litigation we have absorbed from America. So my father just drove down to Newport, arranged for a deferment and made his protest by not shaking hands. Had he been more assertive, had he wielded a kind of authority in his own person – which again means had he been middle class – he could have pushed for the lecturer's dismissal, which is what the man deserved. But he didn't and the college got off lightly.

Over the years and decades we were to become well acquainted with Maindiff Court. My brother was given a regime of lithium and other drugs which helped stabilise his mood swings, but periodically the extremes broke through the barrier created by the drugs and he would be swept away in manic elation before crashing, sometimes in an instant into suicidal depression; or the schizophrenic episodes would return, and then the Masons would be up to their evil games, breaking into the house and giving a knight on a chessboard he had set up half a twist to the left. It was the clearest of messages – 'We've been here. We know all about you. You can't escape.'

It's very difficult for people who aren't trained in the treatment of psychiatric illnesses to learn how to respond to manic depression. You want the individual to return to normal, to be one of the family again. And stabilising drugs like lithium encourage a sense that this has happened. Weeks and months can go by and you are dealing with a person you know; but even the slightest shift between the manic and depressive poles can lead to actions which are unbalanced, which outrage you despite your best efforts not to be outraged. It's like trying to balance a spirit level on an uneven surface – just when you think you have centred the green bubble, it wobbles off to one side and you have to start again. After the upheaval of that summer, and after my brother returned from Maindiff, my parents assumed that, with a period of recuperation, he would be the same as he always had been and that life would return to its small-town routines and certainties. None of us realised that things could never be the same again.

25

In his 'Epilogue' to *Day by Day*, published shortly before he died, Robert Lowell ponders the achievement of his poetry that had depended so much on memory – of his ancestors, his parents, his marriages, his own long battle with manic depression. Was it all in the end just a kind of photography, and not even that, just snapshots 'paralyzed by fact'? 'All's misalliance,' he reflects dejectedly.

But then he rallies – '. . . why not say what happened?' he asks, challenging himself and the reader:

> Pray for the grace of accuracy
> Vermeer gave to the sun's illumination
> stealing like the tide across a map
> to his girl solid with yearning.

Perhaps his own obsession in the poetry with things as they are is not so limited an achievement after all. 'We are poor passing facts,' he concludes, and his own poor health and imminent death would have been in his mind,

> warned by that to give
> each figure in the photograph
> his living name.

Our family photographs are kept in a box made from walnut with mother-of-pearl and perhaps ivory inlay on the lid and around the keyhole. Some of the inlay has fallen out and the casket is shabby now and scabbed. It would have been a fine object in its day, and may have been my grandmother's sewing box that I played with in her room above the shop. The photos are kept in it higgledy-piggledy. Some were once in albums and have been torn out; others have always been loose.

The earliest were taken in Wick at the 'North of Scotland Photographic Rooms' whose motto was *Veluti in Speculum*. There is one of my grandfather, John Henderson Barnie, in a suit of thick cloth, bowler hat in hand, trying to look casual, left thumb jammed into his coat pocket; and another of his father, Donald Barnie, seated in an elaborately carved and tasselled studio chair. Donald must be in his fifties, his son not more than seventeen or so – you can see the thin whisp of his attempt to grow a fashionable moustache. Donald has the bushy grey and white dundrearies of an earlier generation. When he left Caithness, John Henderson never returned, so these photographs must have been taken in 1880-82 when he was about to make the long journey to South Wales and a new life.

Then there is a portrait of John Henderson taken in Swansea at the Studio of Henry A. Chapman, 'Patronized by T.R.H. the Prince & Princess of Wales & the Duke of Edinburgh'; and one of my grandmother, also taken in Swansea but at the Temple Studio of Harrison Goldie. Both are very young – John Henderson still can't generate a proper moustache; my grandmother is perhaps seventeen or eighteen, standing between an ornately carved Victorian table on top of which is a vase that looks like it has been carved as well, and an equally ornate upright chair that might be eisteddfodic but probably isn't. All the photographs are pasted on thick card the size of playing cards.

Were the Swansea photos taken at different studios because John Henderson had not yet met Martha? If he was courting her or if they were engaged, were copies sent to Caithness to show off his sweetheart to his parents?

John Henderson can be followed in photographs; the large-scale head-and-shoulders portrait of a mature man in his thirties, with a full moustache now, and long sideburns. It has been tinted. Two Edwardian wedding photos taken outside the Old Gaol,

Monmouth, one of his eldest daughter May's marriage to Ernie Hodges; one of Jess's marriage to Charles Howes. These would have been taken in about 1903 and 1905. John Henderson has an impressive handlebar moustache; his hair is beginning to recede; he was in his forties. My father is in Jess's photograph, perhaps three or four-years-old, sitting with another boy cross-legged on a coconut-matting doormat; other children are sitting on a rug. He is not in May's photograph.

The last one is from 1912 in his police sergeant's uniform together with a corporal guarding the Rolls's rickety-looking byplane on Monmouth race course. There's a crowd of curious townsfolk, mostly men and boys, all with caps or hats. The photo has been turned into a postcard and must have been on sale in the town. John Henderson was forty-eight; he looks to be in his prime, though three years later he was dead.

The photos come out of the box at random with no sense of historical progression or family relationships. May and Fred Wood standing by the brick wall at the bottom of the garden at Norman Place. May is trying to smile; Fred, cigarette in hand, looks stern. Fred at the head of his horse-drawn baker's van in North Street, with another man, probably his roundsman. A small child, perhaps my cousin Cynthia, sits on the driver's seat. It is late 1920s. My uncle had a bad accident with that van when the horse bolted and tipped the van over on the corner by the convent. The nuns ran out and insisted on taking him in to see to his wounds. There's a photo of the façade of Norman Place with its big, ancient vines of honeysuckle that smelled so overpowering on summer evenings.

My mother is here as a young woman in the late 1920s on the family farm of a schoolfriend, Dorothy Maddocks, out on the road to Monmouth. In all of them they are larking about, having fun.

There are black-and-white Box Brownie snapshots from the early 1950s, of me and my brother, sailing our model yachts in the ornamental gardens at Bournemouth. The yachts are small and disappointing compared to my memory of them. With Lil, Bert and Marjorie Wilcock on a day out at the seaside, perhaps at Barry Island. School portraits of me, year by year, trying to smile, trying to look relaxed. Don, Edgar and Bernard Howes, Jess's sons, in uniform during the Second World War. Don a sergeant and Bernard a lance-corporal in the Army; Edgar in the RAF. Don killed in Italy; Bernard wounded at Arnhem and left with a metal plate in his head. They're smiling, but in a guarded way. Edgar, centre, has his arms folded, head cocked to one side, a natty RAF moustache. He is much more confident than his brothers. Martha Barnie, old but still upright and alert, in a deckchair on an expansive sandy beach. It is summer but she is wearing a long skirt and jacket of heavy woollen material. She looks toward the camera, knitting poised in her hands. 'Smile, Gran,' the cameraman must have said; but she cannot make it. Her face is grim. There are few photographs of Martha smiling.

My brother and myself stand in the back garden at home, hands behind our backs, in short trousers, me in a school blazer and open-necked shirt, my brother in a coat buttoned to the neck and a cap. We are smiling as we were no doubt told to do, my brother genuinely (you can see); my smile is more forced. It is winter because the trellis at our backs has only the naked briars of climbing roses that cascaded in showers of crimson flowers in summer. He is about six, I am about eleven.

There are a few photographs of my father when he was young. One is a studio portrait taken in Weston-super-Mare in 1916 when he was fourteen, standing in a suit with knickerbocker trousers, a tie and a huge white collar. Behind him is a backcloth of waves pounding a beach. His father had been dead for a year. He is serious and you can't see what is in his eyes except perhaps uncertainty. There is one from the early 1930s, a head-and-shoulders studio portrait. It has been crudely cut into an oval and would once have been framed. A more confident man stares out; 1930s steel-framed glasses; a suit jacket; collar skewered with a pin beneath the knot of the tie; a V-necked sleeveless sweater.

There is only one photo from the shop. It shows my father, Nancy Legge, and my mother in close-up, looking down at something, my father laughing. He is wearing his uniform of suit, tightly knotted tie and V-necked sweater. Nancy looks young; it must be from the mid 1950s. You can see a Cadbury's sign partly obscured by my father's head. The snapshot is pale and blurred.

I keep meaning to follow Lowell's injunction and write the names on the backs of the photographs, but don't. Soon there will be no one to identify any of them. Already, for some, it is too late. Who is the young woman holding a Raleigh bicycle? Her face is plump; she has a full woollen hat that comes down over her ears that must have been brightly coloured, a thick cardigan and a skirt that is blowing in the wind. It is winter; you can tell from the trees in the background. The bike looks brand new; it has a carbide lamp, 1930s perhaps, and the bicycle a twenty-first birthday present. It has been pasted in an album and someone has torn it out. Her name will never be recorded by me now; there is no one alive who would know who she was.

There is no one to ask, either, about the studio portrait of two seamen, one a petty officer in a peaked cap and shirt and tie, the other an able seaman, 'HMS Victory' printed on the band of his hat. The small photograph has been embossed 'U.S.A. Studios'. They are young; not more than twenty; possibly they are brothers. It may be from the 1920s. My mother talked of a seaman who was a friend of the Woods who had been wounded in the First World War, leaving his one arm completely numb. When she was a little girl he would let her stick pins in it. But these are too young to have fought in that war. There is no way back to them; they stare out, looking slightly to the right of the camera, an edge of mirth in their eyes as if they can't hold this semi-serious pose another moment.

But perhaps Lowell was wrong. There is a small studio portrait from about 1900 of a young woman, cut by hand into a circle and once set in a frame. Then it was pasted into an album, and finally torn out and kept loose. Someone has written on the back in a hand I don't recognise, 'Thistle Jameson'. She is beautiful, vulnerable, her head leaning toward her right shoulder; around her neck is a double string of pearls. She is perhaps seventeen-years-old.

Then there is an intense young man, hair brushed severely back and pomaded. His three-piece suit is tailored from expensive tweed and his tie has a flamboyant pattern. The corner of a handkerchief falls casually from the breast-pocket of his jacket. There is nothing casual about this man. On the back he has written:

July 1930
To one of my best friends
Andre Gallo. ——

There is no acute accent over the 'e' in Andre.

Was he French or Belgian perhaps? A refugee from the First World War who stayed on? His way of dressing marks him out, as does the fact that his swept-back hair has no parting, something that would have been unthinkable to the shopkeepers in the 1930s. And that handkerchief, ever so carefully arranged in the breast-pocket. Even without the inscription you can tell he 'isn't from round here'. His 'best friend', I'm sure, was a woman.

And who was 'Fredie'. There is an Edwardian postcard among the photographs with a pastel illustration of a young woman in a pale lilac dress of the period and a summer hat, standing in a punt on a lily-strewn lake. In the middle ground there are steps leading up to lawns and formal gardens and the chimneys of a mansion are just discernible over the foliage. She is smiling in a winsome way as she stands ready with the pole. There is a verse printed at the side of the image:

To My <u>Darling Sweetheart</u>

My heart is yours and all my thoughts,
  Will cling to you for ever,
May time but weld our love more deep,
  And nought our two lives sever.

135

On the reverse is written:

With lots of Best Love
for a
Happy Birthday.
Your Ever Loving Boy
Fredie

His name is followed by fifteen kisses. Fredie had a penchant for capital letters and bad verse. The card was not posted; it may have been wrapped with a present or hand-delivered. The only Fred in the family was Fred Wood. When I knew him he was a taciturn, malaria-wracked survivor of Gallipoli, living close to poverty. Could this have been from the days before the war when he was courting May? Before the world closed in on him? Could he have been a carefree 'Fredie' then?

In 'Epilogue', Lowell was talking about art; his photographs were his poems. Yet the metaphor can be inverted. The rather stiff studio portraits of the Victorian and Edwardian eras, the more informal snapshots of the 1950s, are the closest most get to art; the photo album or the line of photos in their frames on the china cabinet, are the portrait galleries where we celebrate those we love and those we have known. Yet the living names survive only as long as there is someone to remember each figure in the photograph with affection. Otherwise, the names scribbled on the backs are as remote and cruel as those carved monumentally on our tombstones.

26

Death came for the shopkeepers and their wives and friends in a myriad ways. Mr Trotman's wild face glimpsed above red blankets on a stretcher at Llanfoist; Don, thin as a skeleton at the table; May Wood yellow with jaundice, taking my hand and placing it on the soft bulge in her side – 'You don't mind, do you, John.' Fred Wood, not long after, in the same bed, my father lifting the old man's head so his lips could suck water from a glass. The stubble on his cheeks was like silver frost.

My mother died alone in intensive care after the third heart attack. My brother had to identify her, even though they knew who she was. For Ted Barnie, it was a slow decline. His heart was as strong as a much younger man's, the family doctor told my mother, but the rest of his body was worn out, was running down.

My brother called me home from Copenhagen and when we arrived, you could see the end was near. He had been sleeping upstairs, but now the flight of stairs that he would once have taken two at a time, was too much for him, so a camp bed had been made up in the dining room. There he lay in his pyjamas with grey Woolsey socks on, a blanket pulled up to his midriff. The bed could be ratcheted up at the back and he lay like this all the time because of the fluid that kept filling his lungs.

We arrived in the evening. My mother and brother were exhausted from staying up with him each night, so I took over, lying down on the sofa parallel to my father. I turned the light out and we lay there sleepless. The curtains were open and through the window I watched the street lamp as it blinked behind the wiry twigs of the mountain ash in the garden.

The rowan was the biggest I have ever seen; it must have been four or five feet in circumference. All through my childhood, it provided shade on the lawn. If you read outside, you could move your chair through the afternoon, following the great shadow-clock of the tree. But power cables ran close outside the garden wall along Priory Road and eventually the tree grew into them. The Electricity Board said it had to be trimmed but what they did was cut an L-shape out of the branches, ruining the beautiful canopy that was orange with berries each autumn. My father pruned the rest of the canopy back, hoping it would regenerate; the tree was too old for such drastic treatment, though, and it died. It was cut back then to the trunk, only a few twigs remaining, which whipped now across the street lamp in the April wind like lashes in a sparkling eye.

I watched it for hours or looked up at the ceiling. Everything in the house was quiet. When my father stirred in the early hours I asked if he would like a cup of tea. 'Aye, that would be nice.' So I went out into the kitchen and turned on the fluorescent light that blinked and flickered into action, making the strong tea with milk that he liked. We sat there drinking it. I was fully clothed and he looked at my ox-blood shoes. 'Those are nice shoes,' he said.

Even in the face of death, we were an inarticulate family. My father never said anything, so far as I know, about his condition, and we all pretended that he was only ill, that he would recover from this. 'Of course you're going to be all right, Ted,' someone would say. And my father would pout, reach for the box of Kleenex that was always at his side now, spitting out the bitter liquid that was drowning him. If my cousins came round, we would talk about him in whispers in the kitchen; the sick man, isolated by our pity, by our inability to talk directly about important things, because, for my parents, life had to be formulated in stories. They had stories about others who had died over the years, but you cannot tell the story of your own death or the death of the person you are looking at, and so there were no words that could be spoken directly between us and my father. When my father said approvingly, 'Those are nice shoes,' therefore, I knew that the words carried a meaning beyond their sense, that they were an expression of his love. We discussed the shoes for a while, and then I turned out the light and we lay there silently, endlessly, until dawn.

One day he wanted to go to the bedroom and I helped him off the camp bed and up the stairs. It was a slow journey; we had to stop again and again as he caught his breath; not like the times when I went with him through Bailey Park, my father on his way to the shop, me on my way to the nuns' primary school. 'Deep breaths!' he'd say, sniffing in the air, the Deri and Rholben shining across at us in the morning light. And I had to run and skip to keep up with his vigorous walk. Now it was as if he was learning to walk all over again, one foot dragged up, then the other, step by step, while I held on firmly to his arm.

I forget what it was he wanted in the bedroom, but on the way out he paused at the mantlepiece and reached toward an ashtray where, among safety pins and copper coins, there was a rusty razor blade. The ashtray was of an olive-green Wedgwood design with a cameo portrait in white of a young woman in classical dress bending over a lyre. He picked up the razor blade and tried to slip it into the breast pocket of his dressing gown. When I saw what he was doing, I guided his hand back to the ash tray; but he tried again, his fingers shaking as he fumbled for the pocket. I made him put the blade back. No words were spoken and we made the slow descent of the stairs.

When I think about this now, I wonder why I didn't let him take the blade. It was the surest sign that he knew he was dying. But we were pretending that he was not. Whether he would have cut his wrists or his throat, there is no way of knowing; nor whether by then he had the strength to do it. My reason for stopping him was wrong, it was a function of our inarticulacy, of the silence that descended on our story-telling family when there were no more stories to tell.

The decline continued and the family doctor called every day.

After about a week when things were getting worse, he gave me two small vials of colourless liquid and told me to give my father a teaspoonful twice a day. I gave him one as soon as the doctor had left and immediately my father fell into a deep sleep. I believe I gave him another later in the day and the same thing happened. This time, though, the sleep got deeper and deeper and it was clear, as the shopkeepers would put it, that he was 'slipping away'. His breathing became slower and shallower; there were long pauses, as if he were holding his breath to listen to something. Several hours passed like this, then his breath began to expel itself in a deep-throated rattle until, at last, there was a flurry of the pulse in his temples and he breathed no more.

I went out to the scullery and unhooked the rusty mirror that he had shaved in every morning while I had known him. The only time my father used the bathroom was for his Sunday bath; otherwise he washed and shaved in the scullery at the kitchen sink, a habit perhaps from the Old Gaol in Monmouth. I took the mirror back to the dining room and placed the glass close to his nostrils; there was no sign of the mist of his breath. I don't know why I did this. I had known he was dead. I put the mirror down and went upstairs to the big front bedroom because I knew I was going to cry, choking it back, almost angrily.

When I went downstairs again, my mother and the rest of the family had moved into the kitchen. Suddenly there was a need for things to do, and I went back into the hall where the telephone was to phone the doctor and tell him what had happened. He came immediately and knelt by the camp bed for a moment, then wrote out and gave me the death certificate. When he had gone I straightened my father's legs, crossed his arms over his chest and drew the blanket up, but not so it covered his face. We agreed that we had better phone the undertaker. There was only one choice, Ted Williams, a small-town man like my father, who knew how things were done. 'Not Ted Barnie!' he had said when I asked him to undertake the funeral.

In his final years, I had watched my father's life as it moved in ever smaller circles. He had reluctantly given up the car; then he came to depend on a walking stick; he no longer went to the Con Club – 'Too old for that now' – and at last his vegetable garden had to be let go. The broad bean plants opposite the kitchen window had been the flags of his last stand.

When you have known someone all your life, there is a trick of the memory which makes you remember first the declining years, the mirror image of your own growth into vigour and maturity. That hand reaching for the razor blade; the unsteady walk down the Hereford Road with the tap-tap of a stick; the querulousness of the old which increases in inverse proportion to their loss of control over their lives.

And you have to fight against this, reach back and pluck out other memories. My father walking briskly through the Park, filling his lungs with the fresh air of the Usk valley; glancing in at the kitchen window and smiling as he passed, terracotta geranium pots in hand, absorbed in the gardening that he loved.

All the old shopkeepers are gone now as are their shops. Shackleton's is still there, but for the rest, the signs have been painted over, often many times, as other traders have come and gone. Percy Jeffries, seedsman, Cliff Scott, my father's rival in the confectionery business, Reg Williams, greengrocer, Ruthers, greengrocer and fishmonger. Up and down Cross Street and Frogmore Street, shops that seemed solid and permanent have disappeared without trace, the lives they encompassed reduced to skeletons and ash. You can see Basil Jones's grocery shop, recreated in Abergavenny Museum, but it is only a shell, old-fashioned and quaint, when set against the bright, bustling supermarkets that dominate the town. To remember the old shopkeepers is to catch sunlight in your hands.

PW